# I WILL NEVER SEE THE WORLD AGAIN

Also by Ahmet Altan

*Endgame*
*Like a Sword Wound*

# I WILL NEVER SEE THE WORLD AGAIN

## THE MEMOIR OF AN IMPRISONED WRITER

### AHMET ALTAN

*Translated by Yasemin Çongar from the Turkish*

*Foreword by Philippe Sands*

OTHER PRESS
*New York*

First published in Great Britain by Granta Books, 2019

The following essays have previously been published in slightly different forms: "The Novelist Who Wrote His Own Destiny" as "I Will Never See This World Again" in the *New York Times* on February 28, 2018; "The Writer's Paradox" in the winter 2017 issue of the *Author*, the journal of the Society of Authors in the UK.

Production editor: Yvonne E. Cárdenas
This book was set in AdobeGaramond.

1 3 5 7 9 10 8 6 4 2

Library of Congress Cataloging-in-Publication Data

Names: Altan, Ahmet, author. | Çongar, Yasemin, 1966- translator. | Sands, Philippe, 1960- writer of foreword.
Title: I will never see the world again : the memoir of an imprisoned writer / Ahmet Altan ; translated from the Turkish by Yasemin Çongar ; foreword Philippe Sands.
Description: New York : Other Press, 2019. | "First published in Great Britain by Granta Books, 2019."
Identifiers: LCCN 2019017340 | ISBN 9781590519929 (paperback) | ISBN 9781635420005 (Ebook)
Subjects: LCSH: Altan, Ahmet—Trials, litigation, etc. | Journalism—Turkey | Political crimes and offenses—Turkey. | Turkey—Politics and government—1980-
Classification: LCC PL248.A525 A6 2019 | DDC 894/.358303 [B]—dc23
LC record available at https://lccn.loc.gov/2019017340

# CONTENTS

# CONTENTS

# FOREWORD

I first met Ahmet Altan in the spring of 2014, at a gathering in Istanbul. The city has long been special to me, as the place where I fell in love thirty years ago, drinking mint tea at a small cafe by the Ortaköy Mosque in the shadow of the Bosphorus Bridge, with the woman I would marry. That spring, Ahmet delivered the first Mehmet Ali Birand Lecture, a now annual event organized by press freedom group P24 to honor the memory of a renowned Turkish journalist. I appreciated Ahmet's lecture, and immediately liked him. He spoke with passion and courage, intelligence and humor on the writer's place in a decent society. Soon we became friends and were often in touch, seeing each other in London and Istanbul.

Four years after Ahmet and I met, in the spring of 2018, I was invited to give the same annual lecture in the same building: the splendid nineteenth-century pile that is the Swedish Consulate General in Beyoğlu on the European side of Istanbul. Ahmet was invited but not able to attend; by then he had been in prison for 590 days. His crime? To speak a few innocuous words on a television program in the aftermath of the failed 2016 coup, which were interpreted as treasonous by President Recep Tayyip Erdoğan's government.

President Erdoğan's crackdown had left Turkey languishing near the bottom of the Reporters Without Borders' World Press Freedom Index. The situation was bad and likely to get worse, even if there was a sense that President Erdoğan's position was not entirely secure in forthcoming elections. The economy was suffering; tourists were staying away. The atmosphere at the Swedish consulate on that spring night in 2018 was one of grim resolve.

My lecture was attended by writers and journalists yet to be arrested. Murat Sabuncu, the editor-in-chief of the *Cumhuriyet* newspaper who had been sentenced in April 2018 to seven-and-a-half years on terror charges but released on bail pending appeal, introduced the proceedings. His speech was an impassioned salute to the many journalists who had been arrested.

I dedicated my lecture to Ahmet. "We know how words are apt to be interpreted in different ways," I said, explaining a point of connection between lawyer and writer, "and we know too that that is their beauty and their danger." The dangerous words spoken by "my dear, absent friend" caused a judge to rule that Ahmet, who was sixty-eight at the time, would spend the rest of his life in prison. "We will never be pardoned and we will die in a prison cell," Ahmet wrote in the *New York Times*, after being sentenced, from his prison cell.

The following day was spent with Yasemin Çongar, who runs P24 and is Ahmet's close friend. We traveled together to the maximum-security prison at Silivri, a two-hour drive from Istanbul. This was where Ahmet was incarcerated, along with his younger brother Mehmet, an economist fired from his position at Istanbul University, where he had taught for thirty years. Yasemin has not been allowed to visit Ahmet – she is permitted ten minutes on the telephone every fortnight – and nor had any foreigner. I was the first allowed in to see Ahmet, because I was acting as a lawyer for the Altan brothers at the European Court of Human Rights in Strasbourg.

The facility was huge and forbidding, holding 11,000 prisoners. Accompanied by a Turkish lawyer, I passed through at least eight security checks and was taken by minibus to Block 9. I was not subjected to the full body search, but was required to have my eyes scanned, to be integrated into "the system." One of the guards was friendly and wanted to talk soccer. We had a short, happy conversation about Arsene Wenger, Mesut Özil (who, much to my sadness, would soon be photographed handing over an Arsenal shirt to President Erdoğan), and what it meant to be Turkish. He had worked there for four years and never encountered a foreigner. "You are the first," he said with a smile.

I met first with Mehmet, who was genial and gentle and had twinkly eyes and a full Karl Marx beard. He was thrilled to talk in French, surprising me with ideas about globalization and the English Luddite movement, on which he had ample time to write. He shared a cell with two other men, one of whom was a former student. Mehmet was perplexed by his situation, and the prospect of spending the rest of his life in prison. A life sentence, he said, is "like living without clocks, in endless time." (Three months later, in the summer of 2018, Mehmet was released.)

Mehmet left. I waited, then Ahmet arrived in our glass-paneled cell. He looked fit. "Weights!" he chortled. We spent most of our thirty minutes roaring with laughter. "No," he said, Turkey had not hit rock bottom yet. "We are a nation of bungee jumpers, and just before we hit the ground we somehow manage to bounce up again." We talked about food, politics, the quality of the grass in my garden in London, and my neighbor, the English magistrate who signed the arrest warrant for Senator Pinochet back in the autumn of 1998. Ahmet marveled again at the idea of justice being dispensed by a judge who was independent. "A miracle," he said.

What did he want his readers to know? I asked. We talked of the judge who sentenced him, a man of "swollen eyelids." Ahmet knew I had a special interest in judges, especially those of the less independent kind. Later I would learn that the name of the man who sentenced Ahmet to life imprisonment for no good reason was Judge Kemal Selçuk Yalçin.

"Did you ever catch his eye?" I inquired.

"Just once: I am the powerful one now, his eyes said, and the power I can exercise will crush you," Ahmet said.

We talked too about his prison memoir, *I Will Never See the World Again*, the remarkable volume which, by a miracle, you hold now in your hands and are about to read. "A rite of passage for any writer to spend time in prison," Ahmet told me. "And you, you will never be a real writer!" We roared with laughter again.

It was quite something to spend a little time with a man sentenced to spend the rest of his life in prison, on trumped-up charges, and who was still able to laugh about it. And something else to leave the prison cell at Silivri with an unexpected feeling of elation, motivated by the sheer towering greatness of Ahmet Altan and the human spirit.

Philippe Sands
London
September 27, 2018

# TRANSLATOR'S NOTE

The essays in this book reached me one by one over a period of seven months between November 2017 and May 2018. They arrived among the personal notes Ahmet had given to our lawyers during their visits to him at Silivri Prison.

Each piece was handwritten on white sheets of paper in blue ink. I would read each piece, read it once again, then immediately type it out on my computer fighting hard not to be overwhelmed with emotion. Once I had the text on the screen before me, I began translating. Typing and then immediately translating each essay in one sitting immersed me in what Ahmet was experiencing, and allowed me to feel his courage and strength at a time when I wasn't allowed to see him.

In the book, Ahmet quotes widely from other authors. In most cases he does so from memory, since in prison he doesn't have access to these texts. Wherever his quotes aren't verbatim, I have remained loyal to Ahmet's memory – to the way his mind has reshaped these sentences in a cell years and miles away from his encounter with them. These recollected quotes are italicized and not sourced. As for quotes from the books Ahmet actually read in prison, these sources are cited on the page.

# I WILL NEVER SEE
# THE WORLD AGAIN

# A Single Sentence

I woke up. The doorbell was ringing. I looked at the digital clock by my side, the numbers were blinking 05:42.

"It's the police," I said.

Like all dissidents in this country, I went to bed expecting the ring of the doorbell at dawn.

I knew one day they would come for me. Now they had.

I had even prepared a set of clothes in an overnight bag so that I would be ready for the police raid and what would follow.

A pair of loose black linen trousers tied with a band inside the waist so there would be no need for a belt, black ankle socks, comfortable soft trainers, a light cotton T-shirt and a dark-colored shirt to be worn over it.

I put on my "raid uniform" and went to the door.

Through the peephole I could see six policemen on the landing, sporting the vests worn by counterterrorism teams during house raids, the acronym "TEM" stamped in large letters on their chests.

I opened the door.

"These are search and arrest orders," they said as they entered, leaving the door open.

They told me there was a second arrest order for my brother Mehmet Altan, who lived in the same building. A team had waited at his door, but no one had answered.

When I asked which number apartment they had gone to, it turned out they had rung the wrong bell.

I phoned Mehmet.

"We have guests," I said. "Open the door."

As I hung up, one of the policemen reached for my phone. "I'll have that," he said, and took it.

The six spread out into the apartment and began their search.

Dawn arrived. The sun rose behind the hills with its rays spreading purple, scarlet and lavender waves across the sky, resembling a white rose petal opening.

A peaceful September morning was stirring, unaware of what was happening inside my home.

While the policemen searched the apartment, I put the kettle on.

"Would you like some tea?" I asked.

They said they would not.

"It is not a bribe," I said, imitating my late father, "you can drink some."

Exactly forty-five years ago, on a morning just like this one, they had raided our house and arrested my father.

My father asked the police if they would like some coffee. When they declined, he laughed and said, "It is not a bribe, you can drink some."

What I was experiencing was not déjà vu. Reality was repeating itself. This country moves through history too slowly for time to go forward, so it folds back on itself instead.

Forty-five years had passed and time had returned to the same morning.

During the space of that morning which lasted forty-five years, my father had died and I had grown old, but the dawn and the raid were unchanged.

Mehmet appeared at the open door with the smile on his face I always find reassuring. He was surrounded by policemen.

We said farewell. The police took Mehmet away.

I poured myself tea. I put muesli in a bowl and poured milk over it. I sat in an armchair to drink my tea, eat my muesli and wait for the police to complete their search.

The apartment was quiet.

No sound could be heard other than the police as they moved things around.

They filled thick plastic bags with the two decades-old laptops I had written some of my novels on and therefore could not bring myself to throw away, old-fashioned diskettes that had accumulated over the years and my current laptop.

"Let's go," they said.

I took the bag, to which I had added a change of underwear and a couple of books.

We left the building. We got into the police car that was waiting at the gate.

I sat with my bag on my lap. The door closed on me.

It is said that the dead do not know that they are dead. According to Anatolian mythology, once the corpse is placed in the grave and covered with dirt and the funeral crowd has begun to disperse, the dead person also tries to get up and go home, only to realize when he hits his head on the coffin lid that he has died.

When the door closed, my head hit the coffin lid.

I could not open the door of that car and get out.

I could not return home.

Never again would I be able to kiss the woman I love, embrace my kids, meet with my friends, walk the streets. I would not have my room to write in, my machine to write with, my library to reach for. I would not be able to listen to a violin concerto or go on a trip or browse in bookstores or buy bread from a bakery or gaze on the sea or an orange tree or smell the scent of flowers, the grass, the rain, the earth. I would not be able to go to a cinema. I would not be able to eat eggs with sausage or drink a glass of wine or go to a restaurant and order fish. I would not be able to watch the sunrise. I would not be able to call anyone on the phone. No one would be able to call me on the phone. I would not be able to open a door by myself. I would not wake up again in a room with curtains.

Even my name was about to change.

Ahmet Altan would be erased and replaced with the name on the official certificate, Ahmet Hüsrev Altan.

When they asked for my name, I would say "Ahmet Hüsrev Altan." When they asked where I lived, I would give them the number of a cell.

From now on, others would decide what I did, where I stood, where I slept, what time I got up, what my name was.

I would always be receiving orders: "stop," "walk," "enter," "raise your arms," "take off your shoes," "don't talk."

The police car was speeding along.

It was the first day of a twelve-day religious holiday. Most people in the city, including the prosecutor who had ordered my arrest, had left on vacation.

The streets were deserted.

The policeman next to me lit a cigarette, then held the packet out to me.

I shook my head no, smiling.

"I only smoke," I said, "when I am nervous."

Who knows where this sentence came from. Nowhere in my mind had I chosen to make such a declaration. It was a sentence that put an unbridgeable distance between itself and reality. It ignored reality, ridiculed it, even as I was being transformed into a pitiful bug who could not even open the door of the car he was in, who had lost his right to decide his own future, whose very name was being changed; a bug entangled in the web of a poisonous spider.

It was as if someone inside me, a person whom I could not exactly call "I" but who nevertheless spoke with my voice, through my mouth, and who was therefore a part of me, said as he was being transported in a police car to an iron cage that he only smoked when he was "nervous."

That single sentence suddenly changed everything.

It divided reality in two, like a Samurai sword that in a single movement cuts through a silk scarf thrown up in the air.

On one side of this reality was a body made of flesh, bone, blood, muscle and nerve that was trapped. On the other side was a mind that did not care about that body and made fun of what would happen to it, a mind that looked from above at what was happening and at what was yet to happen, that believed itself untouchable and that was, therefore, untouchable.

I was like Julius Caesar, who, as soon as he was informed that a large Gallic army was on its way to relieve the besieged occupants of Alesia, had two high walls built – one around the castle to prevent those inside from leaving, and one around his troops to prevent those outside from entering.

My two high walls were built with a single sentence which prevented the mortal threats from entering and the worries accumulating in the deep corners of my mind from exiting, so that the two could not unite to crush me with fear and terror.

I realized once more that when you are faced with a reality that can turn your life upside down, that same sorry reality will sweep you away like a wild flood only if you submit to it and act as it expects you to.

As someone who has been thrown into the dirty, swelling waves of reality, I can say with certainty that its victims are those so-called smart people who believe that you have to act in accordance with it.

There are certain actions and words that are demanded by the events, the dangers and the realities that surround you. Once you refuse to play this assigned role, instead doing and saying the unexpected, reality itself is taken aback; it hits against the rebellious jetties of your mind and breaks into pieces. You then gain the power to collect the fragments together and create from them a new reality in the mind's safe harbor.

The trick is to do the unexpected, to say the unexpected. Once you can make light of the lance of destiny pointing at your body, you can cheerfully eat the cherries you had filled your hat with, like the unforgettable lieutenant in

Pushkin's story "The Shot" who does exactly that with a gun pointing at his heart.

Like Borges, you can answer the mugger who demands, "Your money or your life," with, "My life."

The power you will gain is limitless.

I still don't know how I came to utter the sentence that transformed everything that was happening to me and my perception of it, nor what its mystical source might be. What I do know is that someone in the police car, the person who was able to say he smoked only when he was nervous, is hidden inside me.

He is made of many voices, laughs, paragraphs, sentences and pain.

Had I not seen my father smile as he was taken away in a police car forty-five years ago; had I not heard from him that the envoy of Carthage, when threatened with torture, put his hand in the embers; had I not known that Seneca consoled his friends as he sat in a bath full of hot water and slit his wrists on Nero's orders; had I not read that, on the eve of the day he was to be guillotined, Saint-Just had written in a letter that *the conditions were difficult only for those who resisted entering the grave* and that Epictetus had said *when our bodies are enslaved our minds can remain free*, had I not learned that Boethius wrote his famous book in a cell awaiting death, I would have been afraid of the reality that surrounded me in that police car. I would not have found the strength to ridicule it and shred it to pieces. Nor would I have been able to utter the sentence with secret laughter that rose from my lungs to my lips. No, I would have cowered with anxiety.

But someone whom I reckon to be made from the illuminated shadows of those magnificent dead reflected in me spoke, and thus managed to change all that was happening.

Reality could not conquer me.

Instead, I conquered reality.

In that police car speeding down the sunlit streets, I set the bag that was on my lap onto the floor with a sense of ease, and leaned back.

When we arrived at the Security Department, the car drove through a very large gate at the entrance and started down a winding road. As we descended the slope there was less and less light and the darkness deepened.

At a turn in the road, the car stopped and we got out. We walked through a door into a large underground hall.

This was an underworld completely unknown to the people milling about above. It reeked of stone, sweat and damp. It tore from the world all those who passed through its dirty yellow walls, which resembled a forest of sulphur.

In the drab raw light of the naked lamps every face bore the wax dullness of death.

Plainclothes policemen waited to greet us creatures ripped from the world. Past them, a hallway led deeper inside. Piled at the base of the walls were plastic bags that looked like the shapeless belongings of the shipwrecked swept ashore.

The policemen removed the tie from around the waist of my trousers, together with my watch and my ID.

Here in depths without light, the police, with each of their gestures and words, carved us out of life like a rotten, maggot-laced chunk from a pear, severing us from the world of "the living."

I followed a policeman into the hallway, dragging my feet in laceless shoes. He opened an iron door and we entered a narrow corridor where an oppressive heat grasped me like the claws of a wild beast.

A row of cells behind iron bars ran along the corridor. They were congested with people lying on the floor. With their beards growing long, their eyes tired, their feet bare and their bodies coated in sweat, the boundaries of their existence had melted and they had become a moving mass of flesh.

They stared at me with curiosity and unease.

The policeman put me in a cell and locked the door behind me.

I took off my shoes and lay down like the others. In that small cell filled with people, there was no room to stand.

In a matter of hours, I had traveled across five centuries to arrive at the dungeons of the Inquisition.

I smiled at the policeman who was standing outside my cell, watching me.

Viewed from outside, I was one old, white-bearded Ahmet Hüsrev Altan lying down in an airless, lightless iron cage.

But this was only the reality of those who locked me up. For myself, I had changed it.

I was the lieutenant happily eating cherries with a gun pointing at his heart. I was Borges telling the mugger to take his life. I was Caesar building walls around Alesia.

I only smoke when I'm nervous.

# The First Night in the Cage

I nodded off for a moment. When I opened my eyes, I saw that the staff colonel on the cot across from me and the submarine colonel curled up on a sheet of plastic on the floor were both asleep.

The young village teacher who had been told to sell out his friends laid his prayer rug out between two cots and began his devotions.

In the dim light of the cell I could see his figure – a dark shadow – prostrating itself on the rug.

I had not slept for nearly twenty-four hours, and I was exhausted. My bones ached.

The long black shadows of the iron bars cut through our chests, our faces, our legs and divided us into pieces.

The bare feet of the colonels shone in the cold light seeping in from the corridor, like pieces of white rock.

The colonel across from me groaned in his sleep.

I was in a cage.

In the damp dimness, in the shadows of the iron bars that cut into this dimness, in the young schoolteacher's murmurs of prayer, in the shiny stone-like feet of the colonels, in the moans that came from across the cell, in all of these, there was something more startling than death, something that resembled the empty space between life and death, a no man's hollow which reached neither state.

We were lost in that hollow.

No one could hear our voice. Nobody could help us.

I looked at the walls. It was as if they were coming closer.

Suddenly, I had this feeling that the walls would close in on us, crush and swallow us like carnivorous plants.

I swallowed and heard a groaning noise escape from my throat.

Something was happening.

I felt a battalion of ghosts stir within me. It was as if that famous army of terracotta warriors which the Chinese emperor had built to guard his body after death was coming alive inside me. Each carried with him a different fear, a different horror.

I sat up and leaned my back against the wall.

The heat was brushing my face like a furry animal. My forehead was sweating. I was having difficulty breathing.

This place was so narrow, airless. I wouldn't be able to stay here.

For a moment, I had an irresistible urge to get up, hold the iron bars and shout, "Let me out of here. Let me out of here, I am suffocating."

With horror I realized I was lurching forward.

I clenched my fists as if to stop myself.

I knew that with a single scream I would lose my past and my future, everything I had, but the urge to get myself out of that cage with its walls closing in on me was irresistible.

The terrifying urge to shout and the pressure of knowing that this shout would destroy my whole life were like two mountains colliding and crushing me in between.

My insides were cracking.

The young teacher stood up and put his hands together on his belly; the colonel across from me groaned and turned over onto his other side.

I tucked in my legs and put my arms around my knees.

My vision was getting blurry, the walls were moving.

I wanted to get out of here, I wanted to get out right away, and knowing this was impossible made my brain feel like it had pins and needles, as if thousands of ants were crawling in its folds.

The realization that I was about to embarrass myself intensified my fear even more.

I saw two eyes. Two eyes with a cold, cruel, almost hostile look in them, shiny as glass, like the eyes of a wolf chasing its prey in a rustling forest. Those eyes were inside me, keeping watch over my every move.

I had survived such moments in my youth, moments when I had wandered to the edge of madness. I knew I had to turn back. If I took another step, I would cross the point of no return.

My lungs were rising up to my throat, blocking my windpipe.

The young teacher had again prostrated himself on the prayer rug.

He was muttering a prayer.

He too was begging to be saved.

The colonel lying on the floor groaned in his sleep.

I took a deep breath to push my lungs back down. I gulped some warm water from the plastic bottle I had by my side.

I thought of death.

Instinctively, I was trying to hold on to the idea of death. The eternity of death has the power to trivialize even the most terrifying moments of life.

Thinking that I would die had a calming effect on me. A person who is going to die does not need to fear the things that life presents.

Like everyone else, I was insignificant, what I had been living through was insignificant, this cage, as well, was insignificant, the distress that suffocated me was insignificant, and so too was the evil I had met.

I clung firmly to my own death. It calmed me.

The teacher saluted the angels, turning his head first to the right, then to the left, and finished praying.

He turned around and looked at me.

Our eyes met.

A shy smile appeared on his face as if he were embarrassed – although about what I didn't know.

Moving with difficulty between the two cots, he turned to lie down beside the colonel on the plastic-covered rubber that was on the floor.

His bare feet now shone alongside those of the colonel. The shadow of an iron bar cut through his ankles like a black razor. I saw two feet attached to nothing. I was going to die one day. What I was living through was insignificant. The eyes inside me were shut. The wolf was gone. I wasn't going to lose my mind.

During a scorching heatwave, when crops catch fire, a circle is drawn around the blaze and the grain along that circle is deliberately set alight before the flames can reach it. Once the fire arrives at the circle it stops, as there is nothing left there to burn. They use fire to put out fire.

I had surrounded and extinguished the fire of terror, which life had lit in a cage, with the fire of death.

I knew that my life from now on would be a series of opposing fires. I would surround those started by my jailers with the fires of my mind.

Sometimes death will be the source of the latter; sometimes the stories I write in my mind; sometimes the pride that won't let me leave behind a name stained by cowardice; sometimes it will be sex releasing the wildest fantasies; sometimes peaceful reveries; sometimes the schizophrenia unique to writers who twist and tweak the truth in their red-hot hands to create new truths; sometimes it will be hope.

My life will pass fighting invisible battles between two walls; I will survive by hanging on to the branches of my own mind, at the very edge of the abyss, and not giving in to the disorientating inebriety of weakness, even for a moment.

I had seen the monstrous face of reality.

From now on I would live like a man clinging to a single branch.

I didn't have the right to be scared or depressed or terrified for a single moment, nor to give in to the desire to be saved, to have a moment of madness, nor to surrender to any of these all-too-human weaknesses.

A momentary weakness would destroy my entire past and future – my very being.

If I were to tire and let go of the branch I was holding, it would be fatal; I would fall to the bottom of the abyss and become a mess of blood and bones.

Would I be able to endure the days, weeks, months and years of swinging in the air unable to let go of the branch for even an instant?

If I were to let go and break to pieces in the abyss of weakness, I would lose not only my past and future but also the strength that enables me to write.

Because the prospect of being cut off from the precious lode of writing scared me more than anything; that fear would suppress all other fears and give me the ability to endure. Courage would be born of fear.

Now that the fear of losing my mind which had momentarily licked my insides had passed, together with the distress caused by the heavy feeling of suffocation, a tense fatigue took hold of my body.

The teacher, like the colonel, was fast asleep now. The restless movement of those feet cut off from the ankles had stopped.

Though tired enough to pass out, I couldn't sleep. It was as if even sleep itself was too exhausted to come and take me.

When the police had taken me from my apartment, I had thrown in my bag a book I had recently ordered on medieval Christian philosophers, thinking it would have entertaining and diverting stories about their lives.

To escape what I was living through, to rest and relax a little, I would take refuge in what they had endured.

These philosophers struggled to resolve the secrets of their personal lives while still daring to unravel the mysteries of the universe. They experienced an innocent helplessness before the question "what is life?," even though they had written thousands of pages on the subject. This, it had always seemed to me, was an amusing summary of the human condition.

In that dim light, as my cagemates moaned and groaned, I opened the book.

I had hoped reading would calm me and put me to sleep. I was wrong.

The book did not consist of entertaining biographies. Instead, it recounted the philosophers' rather compelling views.

And Saint Augustine, of course, was the first one to greet me.

This bear of a man prays sincerely to be rid of the burden of sexuality, yet begs God not to be in a hurry because he is having a good time. He persists in trying to find a reasonable explanation for why God, being "absolutely good," would create such grave evil. Augustine wakens in me a sense of tenderness that contrasts with his stature and significance.

I began to read.

That a man locked in a cage would find himself with no alternative but to read about why God created evil seems part of life's unfathomable facetiousness.

This time, reading Augustine angered me. He says that God had reason to create torture, persecution, sorrow, murder and the cage they locked me up in, along with the men who locked me up in it: all this evil, says Augustine, was the result of Adam acting with "free will" and eating the apple.

I was in a cage because a man had eaten an apple.

The man who ate the apple was God's own Adam, made by his own hands; the man who was locked in the cage was me.

And Augustine was asking me to be thankful for this?

I grumbled as if he stood before me, shoddily dressed, with his big balding head, long beard and charming smile.

"Tell me," I said, "what is the bigger sin – a man eating an apple or punishing all of humanity with torture because a man ate an apple?"

I added furiously, "Your God is a sinner."

The colonel across from me turned to his side, groaning; the shadow of the bar cut off half his face.

"I am paying for your God's sins."

My eyes were burning from fatigue, from lack of sleep. A stupor-like slumber was dragging me down.

The colonel across the room moaned.

I looked up and saw that he was awake, and crying.

While he was in jail, his three-year-old child was in hospital, grappling with death.

I turned and faced the wall so he wouldn't know I had seen him cry.

I was never going to let the branch go. Not even for a moment.

As I fell asleep I thought of that little girl grappling with death.

"Is an apple worth all of this?" I wondered.

The Mirror and the Doctor

Has your face ever suddenly disappeared?

The face you see dozens of times a day in mirrors and shop windows, on shiny surfaces and the screen of your phone, every curve and wrinkle of which you are so familiar with; has this face ever been erased from life?

I don't suppose even a single day passes without you seeing your own face.

You see it so often that you forget how the sight of it, how making eye contact with yourself, is a small miracle.

On my first morning in the cage, I woke up to the rattling of a shopping trolley.

The policemen were distributing cheese sandwiches fresh from the freezer and small plastic bottles of water.

The sandwiches were frozen.

Then they opened the gates of our cages.

At the end of the corridor of cells there was an iron door; when you pushed it open, two sinks appeared.

There was no mirror above them, only the wall.

Like everyone else, I am so used to seeing my own reflection first thing in the morning that I looked straight ahead, expecting to see my face.

It had disappeared.

In that instant I felt as if I had crashed into the wall.

Like everyone else, I looked around, searching for myself.

I wasn't there.

It was as if I had been erased from life, tossed away.

Looking at that bare wall drove home what it means to see your own reflection. However many thousands of times mirrors appear as a literary metaphor, the reality is more significant than a metaphor could ever be.

The mirror shows you to you, it confirms your being. The distance between you and the mirror creates a field that belongs only to you, a field that surrounds you, is yours, somewhere no one else can trespass.

Without a mirror, that field also disappears.

It feels like everyone and everything is sticking to you, crowding you.

You can see your hands, your arms, your legs, your feet, but not your face.

Without a face, all those arms, hands, feet, legs resemble the body of a half-ape–half-bird found in the Madagascar forests.

When your face has disappeared, you can't even be sure if those hands and feet really belong to you.

In the cages there was no mirror, no piece of reflecting glass, no shiny surface.

Whoever had designed that place had done so knowingly. He must have thought that the people in that building undergoing fierce interrogation would break more easily having lost their faces.

Like me, everyone was searching for their face.

Some stared into the plastic water bottles, but the plastic did not reflect the light.

By simply putting away the mirrors, they had erased us from life.

I thought of Narcissus and the pool in Oscar Wilde's story.

When Narcissus died, the sweet waters that had filled the pool in which he used to look at himself every day turned to tears.

The tears said to the pool, *We do not wonder that you should mourn . . . he . . . would lie on your banks and look down at you . . . in the mirror of your waters he would mirror his own beauty.*

*But I loved Narcissus because . . . in the mirror of his eyes I saw my own beauty mirrored,* answered the pool.

Even a pool wants to look at itself, yet our ties to our selves were broken.

Even washing one's own face was difficult without a reflection. When you raised your cupped palms that were filled with water to splash your face, there was a worry that you might miss altogether.

Under the sinks there was a large plastic barrel spilling over with used, crumpled pieces of dirty paper which were also scattered around on the floor.

Because it was a religious holiday, most of the cleaners were on leave, so empty paper towel rolls were not replaced with new ones, the floors were not cleaned and everywhere was filthy.

There were two toilets near the sink.

I had never seen a toilet like that.

It had wooden swinging doors like the bars in old Westerns. The top and the bottom parts of the door were not there.

There was a shower stall near the toilets. It too had swinging doors.

There was no place to hang your clothes.

When you took a shower, you were supposed to hang your clothes and towel over the swinging doors.

The floor was covered in thick gunk.

I was finally beginning to stink, so I gave in and took a shower. Because I didn't dare to step barefoot on the floor, I washed myself with my socks on. Later, I discovered the difficulty of putting on dry clothes while wearing wet socks.

After we had washed our hands and faces we went back to our cages. We ate our frozen sandwiches and drank our bottles of water.

My cagemates and I began to talk.

All of the colonels in the lockup were sailors and all were classmates who had graduated the same year from the Navy War College.

The funny thing was that these men were not the coup

plotters but the officers who had been appointed to replace those who had been arrested.

Then one of their classmates had pointed the finger at them.

It seems there was a huge epidemic of double-crossing in the armed forces in those days, with officers informing on each other without mercy.

When a friend of this group of officers had ratted on them, the police had rounded up all of the navy colonels who had graduated in the same year.

Most of them were staff colonels.

They were well educated; they all had PhDs, in a variety of subjects, and promising careers.

They were confused and uneasy but, being childhood friends, they turned our corridor into a military school dorm; they picked on each other, joked and laughed as their hands curled around the iron bars.

We were settling into a strange zone of laughter and agony as one by one their souls crystallized under pressure. In just an hour, the reticent, the joker, the neurotic, the thick-skinned and the ambitious all made an appearance.

Apparently, the one with the most brilliant career among them was the staff colonel who slept across the room from me. He had served abroad, traveled the world, finished first in all his missions and maneuvers, and just as he was waiting to be made general, found himself barefoot in a police holding cell.

He had nurtured big dreams, but all that changed in one night with the handcuffs they put around his wrists.

All the officers there had taken the same slap in the face, experienced the same jolt, but the one who lost most was the staff colonel because he had had the biggest dreams.

He grieved both for his hospitalized daughter and his future that was fast disappearing.

The submarine colonel, on the other hand, was a happy, carefree sort of chap. Though clever, he did not want to become a staff officer; that wasn't his ambition.

"How is life in a submarine?" I asked him.

He laughed and said, "Worse than here."

He was used to getting lost in enclosed spaces.

As the days passed, the subject of food began to dominate the conversation.

We were starving. In the mornings, they gave us a frozen sandwich, at noon, tinned peas, and at dinner, stuffed vine leaves, also tinned.

We were given no tea, no coffee, no cigarettes and no other food.

During the twelve days I stayed there we ate cheese sandwiches, tinned peas and stuffed vine leaves.

Truly, this was a slimming diet: I lost fifteen pounds in twelve days; others, depending on the time they had spent there, lost twenty, even thirty pounds.

We dreamed of food.

One day when the policemen opened the gates of the cages for us to walk up and down in the corridor, as we started pacing in a single row, I said, "Let's each name the dish we miss most."

The names of dishes began exploding in a cascade of fireworks. "Adana kebab," "İskender kebab," "white bean stew," "fish and arugula," "lahmadjun," "pastrami," "dumplings."

It was as if we were devouring the names we recited – we shouted with such a huge appetite that it seemed we were living out some sort of food orgy. The name of each dish was followed by a "wow" of appreciation and desire.

After such joyful moments, a dead weight would descend on us. The cable of energy that fed a protective shield of childish games, jokes, teasing and happy memories was cut and reality seeped in:

We were locked up in cages. Our futures did not look all that bright.

"But we didn't do anything," the staff colonel across from me said in a murmur. He was on vacation in Antalya with his family on the night of the coup, he told us once again.

The submarine colonel responded in a tone of indifference, "These guys would send us to prison first, then expel us from the military."

The staff colonel objected:

"Why would they expel us? What did we do?"

These men had been in the military before they had even become adults, and the possibility of expulsion sent shivers down their spines.

I usually kept out of their conversations. I either read the musings of Saint Augustine and Thomas Aquinas on evil or daydreamed.

I repeated to myself the best-known, the most commonplace truth of life with utter respect for the cliché: "Time passes, everything changes."

I remembered words from Elias Canetti: *When you touch time with the tips of your fingers, it laughs all at once and scatters like dust.*

Time did not laugh here.

It did not laugh even when I touched it with my fingertips.

But it was true that it turned into dust. I could feel it in my mouth, in my nose, in my throat. I chewed and swallowed each speck of dust.

Each speck of dust I swallowed confirmed the cliché: "Time passes."

During one of those dead hours we heard a policeman shout:

"Get ready! You are going to the doctor's."

"What's happening?" I asked.

"They're taking us to the doctor's so they can prove we weren't tortured," the young teacher said.

I was going to go out into the sun, into the light.

All at once, I became uneasy.

I didn't want to go into the sun, into the light. The idea of leaving the cage frightened me.

Like a crab buried in mud, I had buried myself in the cage, in my daydreams and in time. I had made myself a nest there, away from the world.

Once I was out in the sun, in the light, in life again, this "nest" would be destroyed. I didn't know if I would find the strength to rebuild it when I returned.

I would have stayed put in that cage if I could have done, but I had to move. I stood up with everyone else.

My linen trousers, without the cord around the waist, kept slipping down and exposing me. This was not an outfit in which I could socialize.

One of the colonels saw my dilemma.

"Let's make you a belt," he said.

"How would you manage to do that?"

He peeled the label off a plastic water bottle and, by twisting the paper, turned it into a short piece of string, which he put through the belt loops of my trousers and tied at the front.

The trousers stayed around my waist.

We exited the cells, walking between two rows of uniformed policemen, and made our way toward a bus with steel mesh covering its windows.

Perhaps no other scenario could make a person look more like a wretched criminal than being made to walk in a ragged human chain of wrinkled trousers, dirty undershirts, misshapen slippers, unkempt hair and un-trimmed beards.

In the mayhem of this human effluent trying to adjust an agitated mess of strides to orders barked by the police, in the confusion brought about by failing to get used to this new situation and thus not knowing who you were, all the visible characteristics that made you *you* – your expressions, your gestures, your voice, your walk – were disappearing.

I could see how pitiful all of us looked in the midst of that grayish slurry.

We got on the bus. It grunted its way forward, passed through the rows of parked cars and left the Security Department's yard, turned right and stopped in front of the hospital, which was just around the corner.

There was a tiny square near the hospital. A small crowd waited there under the scorching sun.

At once I saw in that crowd the faces I loved and missed.

Craning their necks and squinting hard, they tried to see between the shadows of the steel mesh whether I was on the bus or not.

I was overjoyed at the sight of them.

To appreciate what a joy it is to see your loved ones, even at such a distance, you need to sit with a paper belt around your waist in a police bus with steel mesh across its windows.

We love and get used to loving.

It is sometimes only possible to understand how great the love is that lies beneath that habit when the habit is broken in such a loutish way.

I was waving with excitement so that they would see me. Their seeing me at that moment was the most important thing in my life; I was thrashing about, but they couldn't pick me out from among the shadows on the bus.

I couldn't move as much as I wanted to as the policemen were constantly ready to step in.

My loved ones couldn't see me.

At that moment, nothing in life was more important than being seen by them.

One of the colonels sitting in the front said, "Move forward, it looks like your family is here," and gave me his seat.

Regardless of any differences in their ideas, convictions and beliefs, there is always a solidarity between people who meet in such dire circumstances. Everyone helped one another. We stuck to each other like a flock of starlings that had encountered predatory birds.

I went to the front.

I waved.

They saw me.

First, they smiled and waved happily.

Then I saw ripples move upward from my daughter's kneecaps, and then those waves burst from her eyes in the form of tears.

She was trying to contain herself but couldn't. Her whole body was shaking.

My son held her and pressed her to his chest.

I looked at them.

I knew the deep wounds that opened inside me at that moment would never heal.

I knew all too well what they must have felt when they saw their father on a bus covered with steel mesh in the middle of a miserable crowd.

After they had arrested my father, my brother Mehmet and I went to his hearing in a military court.

In the courtroom inside the Selimiye Barracks the two of us were the only audience. By coincidence, we both wore dark blue suits that day.

The following morning a right-wing newspaper printed a large photograph of us on its front page implying that there was a "hidden message" in our donning the same color suits.

Everything changes on earth, but stupidity and meanness never change.

My father was in the defendant's chair. Two gendarmes were standing at either side.

Then my father stood to deliver his defense. He spoke with a strong, impressive voice that resonated along the stone-walled corridors of the military barracks. The courtroom began to fill up gradually as officers left their rooms and came to listen to my father.

The chief judge wanted to shut my father up. My father wouldn't shut up.

The judge shouted: "Make him sit down." Two gendarmes pushed down on my father's shoulders and pressed him into his seat.

I never forgot the helplessness and anger I felt at that moment. My hatred of despots and putschists would never go away.

Seeing my children's pain now, I not only understood how they felt but also felt again the same helplessness and anger that had overtaken me years ago as I watched my father.

To try and calm their distress, I smiled and signaled that I was fine. In reality, I was wondering how I looked.

I was worried that if I appeared overly tired and unkempt it would add to their distress.

They made us get off the bus in and enter the hospital in single file.

A receptionist sat before a computer and asked everyone for their ID numbers and names.

When it was my turn, she asked me my ID number.

"I don't know," I said.

I heard behind me the scornful voice of the young policeman with an ostentatious hairstyle: "Look at him, the big-name writer, he doesn't even know his ID number!"

I had become an absolute "nobody" in the eyes of a young police officer because I didn't know my ID number.

That is how they had taught him to live: first of all, memorize your number.

When I entered the doctor's room, he greeted me. "How are you, Ahmet Bey?" he asked.

"I am fine, thank you."

The doctor pointed toward a curtained door at the back of the examination room.

"There is a mirror back there, you can look if you'd like."

Clearly he knew the importance of mirrors, the impact of one's face disappearing.

I immediately opened the curtain and looked in the mirror that hung above the sink. My face was there, looking at me. I had found my missing piece. I was complete. I had left the body of the half-ape–half-bird creature and become human again.

I didn't look as exhausted as I had feared.

That made me rather happy.

My loved ones would not have to feel even more distress.

"Have they assaulted or tortured you?" asked the young doctor.

"No."

"Do you have any other complaints?"

"Sometimes I have difficulty swallowing at night."

"Let me write you a prescription."

"Are you an ear, nose and throat specialist?"

"No, I am an orthopedist."

"Then how do you know about throat medicine?"

"I have the same problem, that's how."

After everyone had been examined by the doctor, they took us back to the bus again in a single line. As I was getting on the bus I turned and waved: "I am fine."

The bus moved and we entered the Security Department's yard.

Our loved ones were grasping the bars of the wrought-iron fence surrounding the yard as the bus left them behind.

They became further and further away. They looked so small.

I was looking at them through the steel mesh on the bus windows. As we moved further away, the stinging pain inside me worsened.

They put us into the cages again.

There was silence in the lockup.

Some, like me, had seen their loved ones outside the hospital, but some had not. We were longing for those we had seen, while those others were longing for those they could not see.

Nothing disturbed our silence until dinner.

Everyone took refuge in his own loneliness.

In the evening, the policemen distributed cans of stuffed vine leaves.

As we ate we began talking.

We had reburied ourselves in the muddy world of the cage and had settled there.

I asked the young teacher who had been in the lockup for four weeks, "Haven't they interrogated you yet?"

Two weeks before, they had taken him for interrogation at dawn and had told him this: "Everyone is trying to save his own backside. You go away now and think a while. Give us some names. Save your backside."

"I can't give them any names. I can't harm anyone," he said.

When I woke up briefly in the night, I saw him leaning against the wall reading the Qur'an.

The following day they took us to see the doctor again.

This time I was prepared for seeing my loved ones.

They were prepared for me too.

They smiled, and I waved to them with joy.

A somewhat overweight female doctor was on duty.

"Been assaulted?"

"No."

"I will examine you."

"No assault."

"I have to examine you."

We went behind the curtain. I saw myself in the mirror. I had a face. I existed.

"Pull down your trousers," said the doctor.

I felt like saying "You first," but I managed to restrain myself.

I pulled down my trousers.

The woman was looking at my legs and I was looking at her; we were just standing there.

That unforgettable scene in Steinbeck's *Sweet Thursday* came to my mind.

Doc goes to visit Suzy, who has moved into an empty boiler in a vacant lot. As he crawls into the boiler on all fours, holding flowers in one hand, he thinks to himself, "A man who can do this with dignity need never again fear anything."

A man who can stand with dignity before a woman with his trousers around his knees need never again fear anything.

Then she said, "You can pull up your trousers."

As I was leaving I asked the doctor what her area of specialism was.

I'll file her response under "unforgettable."

"Gynecology."

# The Teacher

*Suddenly snow began to fall. Everything turned white. The road ahead of us disappeared and we couldn't tell where the road ended and the fields began. The snow hitting the windows of the minibus accumulated so fast we had difficulty seeing outside. The driver said, "I am turning back. If we stick around here any longer, the road home will be closed too and we'll be stranded."*

*"You go back. I'll walk to the village," I said as the minibus maneuvered to turn round. I got out of the vehicle.*

So began the most surprising story of happiness I have ever heard.

The air and the light in our cage never changed. Each minute was the same as the last. It was as if a tributary of the river of time had hit a dam and formed a lake. We sat at the bottom of that motionless pool.

In the depths of that turbid mass of water we were as worthless as an empty cigarette packet or the coins a passing drunk takes out of his pocket and tosses away while crossing a bridge.

We couldn't tell in which direction time flowed. Sometimes it flowed toward the past, toward our memories. Sometimes it flowed toward the future and our worries. But more often it stagnated in this strange-smelling gloom.

We knew each element of that smell: the smell of stone, the smell of iron, the smell of oppressive heat, the smell of human skin, the smell of unclean toilets, the smell of waste paper, the smell of the absence of light.

But the sour and nervous smell that was the combination of them all put together was an unknown and depressing stench for all of us.

Inactivity fatigued us.

The only way to move was with the voice – by talking and telling.

Anyone on earth who finds a listener has a story to tell. What is difficult to find is not the story, but the listener. I was the listener in that cage.

With that eerie, unreliable instinct possessed by writers, I listened to everything they told me and recorded it in my memory in order to sift through it all later.

The tellers perhaps thought that what they were saying would soon be forgotten. They didn't know the ease with which writers commit the sin of not forgetting.

The colonels had a rich repertoire of stories. They were talkative. The young teacher, however, didn't talk much. He either listened to the others or read the Qur'an.

After the police had told him to go away, to think things over and give them a few names, they left him to himself in the cage.

As happened with so many others in those cells, his mind ebbed and flowed: should he save himself by becoming an informant and shopping his acquaintances, or should he avoid sullying himself with such baseness but pay the price of purity and be sentenced to rot in prison?

Every now and then he said, "I cannot give them anyone's names, I cannot be that vile," but he couldn't bring himself to say to the police, "I have nothing else to tell you."

He was struggling with the bitter consequences of this inner agitation.

When he spoke with us, he would only talk about his time in that snowed-in Kurdish village, a time he described as "the happiest years of my life."

*Suddenly snow began to fall . . .*

His adventures had started when he had been given a teaching post in the Southeast in a pro-government village controlled by local guards.

He had rented a house in the nearby town with a couple of friends who were also teachers. He went to the village in the morning and returned at night.

On that morning when the snowstorm began, he got off the minibus and started making his way through the snow.

He walked for hours, got lost a few times, even collapsed once at the bottom of a tree, feeling cold and exhausted. With one last effort, he continued to walk, and arrived in the village toward the evening almost frostbitten.

He went to the village headman's house, rang the doorbell and made a declaration to the headman, who listened with an astounded look on his face. "From now on I will stay in the village."

It was clear that earlier that day, at the very moment he said, "I'll get off here and walk," he had made a life-changing decision.

There are such turning points in people's lives, moments that change their paths forever, but few people have a clear-eyed grasp of them.

The young teacher had etched into his memory all the details of the moment he had decided to change his life.

He had poured his heart and soul into that decision.

He never talked about his emotions in the moment he made that decision, nor how he felt about it after what came later.

All his feelings were locked behind the sentence "Those were the happiest years of my life," and he didn't allow anyone to see them.

His silence opened a vast, fertile field before me, one I could fill with my own thoughts, predictions and dreams.

When he decided to live in the village, when he said, "I'll get off here," he must have known that, by doing so, he would cut all ties with his life outside that mountain hamlet, that intense solitude and harsh conditions awaited him.

In that moment he walked away from life.

He walked away from all pleasures, all entertainment, all conversation with friends, from idly roaming the crowded city streets, from seeing a shirt he liked in a shop window and buying it. Above all, in that moment he walked away from love and the possibility of finding a life partner, and he dedicated himself to something else entirely.

That was the moment he dedicated himself to other people.

He left his own self and dedicated his being to something else, just as a monk, a mahatma, a saint would.

In that lightless cage I could imagine myself in his place and feel what he must have felt at the moment he got out of the minibus.

I didn't only feel what he felt, however. Like Süskind's protagonist who steals others' scents, I took the young teacher's adventures and filled them with my own emotions to weave myself a dream cloak from his memories, a cloak in which I could wrap myself up and hide.

I was out in the snow. I was freezing. I could feel in every particle of my being an acute sense of exuberance that came from having cracked the shell around me with my own will, from sailing to a state without boundaries, leaving all worldly pleasures behind and being dispersed like snowflakes into infinity.

I had the dizzying experience of getting rid of my

wings, those made of life and death, and flying wingless into infinity.

Leaving my body in the cage, I flew around like a snowflake smiling in a blizzard.

Becoming a snowflake had such a delicious, burning zest to it, a sense of bleeding and breaking as if one was giving birth to one's new self.

My time in the midst of that whiteness was one of the happiest moments of my life. It was a borrowed happiness, but it was happiness.

I don't know whether the young teacher really experienced that moment in this way or whether these were merely the fairy-tale journeys of my mind, relishing its dreamy escape from the oppressive feeling of being stuck in that cage. But that is what happened to me as I listened to him.

The shared life of what he had experienced and what I dreamed ended there.

I could feel the instant when he got out of the minibus: a person imploding with what felt like a "Big Bang" to create a new person, a new life, a new universe from within himself was not hard for me to empathize with.

I could feel in my own soul that moment of mystical contemplation.

I could easily slip away from the sticky heat of that dark cage and walk through the blizzard, feeling the snow on my face, the tingling in my fingers, the excitement mixed with fear. I could feel with a cramp in my stomach the eerie inner journey of leaving a life behind and jumping into the void in search of another life.

But I could neither feel nor understand the "happiness" of the three years that followed.

On that snowy night, the village headman asked the teacher at his door to come in and sit near the stove, fed him a meal and served him coffee.

After coffee the headman said, "There are no vacant houses in the village."

Determined to live there, the teacher asked, "What should we do?"

The headman thought for a while.

"There is a room full of old furniture next to the mosque. If you wish, we can talk to the imam and you can stay there."

"All right," said the teacher.

As he was eager to settle in his new home as soon as possible, they took a torch with them and made their way to the mosque through the snow in the freezing cold and found the imam.

The imam, not wanting to offend the headman or the teacher who came at night to his door, came out, walked with them and unlocked the room.

It was a small room full of broken crates, coffin lids, caskets and torn old rugs, with no running water or electricity, and no glass visible on its frozen windows, just an opaque whiteness.

The imam went to his house and brought back a metal wood-burning stove. They lit it and the room got a bit warmer. The imam and the headman left.

The teacher put one of the torn rugs on the floor, wrapped himself in his coat and fell asleep among the coffins.

During his three years in this room with no toilet, no bath and no kitchen, he lived the happiest days of his life.

He cooked his meals on the wood-burning stove and did his laundry in a washtub that he found.

As he talked about those days, a twinkle that resembled the light of a comet flowing back through time toward the past appeared.

Even in our dim cage, the light of happiness could be seen on the teacher's face.

The young man who lay alone wrapped in his coat on

a torn rug he had placed on ice-cold stone floors had found happiness there, and he was now embracing those memories in an effort not to turn into an informant in this police lockup where he was spending perhaps the most difficult days of his life.

I thought hard, trying to solve the mystery of his unprecedented happiness of three years.

What was it that gave happiness to this young man as he spent three years of his life without love, without the companionship of a woman, all by himself in a room that he shared with coffins in an isolated hamlet on a snowy mountain?

Was it the sensation I imagined it to have been?

Had the young teacher managed to feel that sense of ecstasy moment after moment for years, like a monk, a saint, while I could only conjure up a single moment of it now?

Or was it only because his days in the village seemed so secure, given the darkness of his present misfortune, that he now remembered that time as a period of "happiness"?

Or perhaps it was the affection and trust of the people in that village that had made him happy?

Had he filled the void created by the lack of a woman's love with the affection of an entire village?

The warmth of a woman didn't exist in this story of happiness. In its place was a wider, broader, and therefore less intense and less heated, reliable kind of affection.

Was it this communal affection that was to him unforgettable?

Could a village's affection make a man as unforgettably happy as a woman's love?

I couldn't find the answer to any of these questions among the teacher's memories.

During those days we spent together in the cage, he didn't talk about his life either before or after his time in the village.

I knew nothing about his life except for his time in that village. It was as if the only period he could remember from his past was those three years. Nothing else had left so deep a mark on him.

Whenever he drew open the curtains of his life, we always saw the same village stage set; the light of his memory did not illuminate any other scene.

When he wasn't talking about the village, he was either reading the Qur'an or praying, or else he would mutter as if talking to himself: "I cannot give away anyone's names, I cannot be that vile."

Sometimes when I woke up at night I saw him praying. This young man's story of happiness brought to my mind what Brodsky said in his book about Venice. *The smell of frozen seaweed* was synonymous with happiness for Brodsky.

A smell completely unknown to me made him think of "absolute happiness."

The smell of frozen seaweed, an isolated village, a walk in the snow, walking away from life . . . All those could lead to happiness.

How could Brodsky and the village teacher, two people entirely unlike each other, roam around in different depths of life, take dissimilar paths and arrive at the same word, "happiness"?

I wanted to understand this.

In a cage that objectified unhappiness, I was thinking about what happiness was. Like a blind alchemist searching for the spell that turns copper into gold, I was trying to find the secret that turned "frozen seaweed" and "coffin lids" into joy.

I knew copper, I knew gold, and I could see copper turning into gold before my very eyes. There had been times when I too had turned copper into gold, though I was unable to identify the magical formula.

Like a fortune-teller looking at his crystal ball in the dark, I was looking at the word I held in my hands: happiness. How brilliant and charming it was. And how strongly it resisted my efforts to wheedle out its secret. Each time I laid my eyes on it, it looked different.

Copper turns into gold, I said at last, but everyone has his own method of transforming copper – there is no general formula for it; the formula is inside each alchemist, hidden in his very soul, in his own past.

The young teacher struggling with himself in that cage taught me this.

I didn't give him back the moment I had borrowed from him, that moment of stepping out of the minibus in the snow. It stayed with me. It became mine.

During many nights when the heat that crawled among the sharp shadows of the iron bars dug its teeth into my flesh like a furry crocodile, I got out of the vehicle and walked in the snow. I was cold with happiness.

I made gold from copper, not knowing how I had done it.

Then one morning they took away the young teacher and put him in prison.

He had not given them any names.

The Cemetery of Pink Folders

It's almost morning but still dark outside. My brother Mehmet and I are on the seventh floor of the courthouse, waiting in a corridor that shines with fluorescent lights and mica that remind me of the coffee shops in rural America. We are surrounded by a dozen or so policemen.

We've both lost weight. Our faces bear the marks of a lack of good nutrition and sleep.

Yesterday evening we were taken out of the cages at the police lockup where we have been kept for twelve days and brought to the courthouse. They first put us in a waiting room on the ground floor of the building with iron bars around it and wooden benches against its walls.

We sat on the benches. There was another defendant

with us, a man we were meeting for the first time in our lives but with whom we would be put on trial.

A television mounted on the wall opposite us was playing a Turkish soap opera. The quality of the picture was very bad and there was a lot of static. On a notice-board near the TV set was a warning: "No one is to touch the television except for the television attendant."

We waited there for over three hours.

Then the policemen came and took me to the prosecutor's room. My lawyer joined us.

The prosecutor whom I was taken to see was the man who had first detained Mehmet and me on the charge that we had given "subliminal messages" on a TV show the night before the attempted military coup of July 15, 2016.

It was a small room.

The prosecutor started his interrogation. He didn't ask me a single question about the military coup, the putschists or the "subliminal messages" we were said to have given.

Instead, his questions had to do with the newspaper we had founded ten years ago, the one I had edited for five years until my resignation in 2012.

At one point, he said, "We have established that the putschists are linked to this newspaper."

"Where is the evidence for this?" I asked.

He uttered a sentence that he must have learned from Hollywood and been eager to use someday:

"I ask the questions here."

"You ask the questions, but when you say you have established a fact, you must show the evidence for it."

Of course, no such evidence was ever produced, neither that day nor later.

The prosecutor was extremely restless. He kept pacing the room. Every now and then, he would briefly return to his armchair before getting up again.

Halfway through the interrogation, his ear started bleeding. He stuffed it with a tissue in an effort to stop the bleeding, but kept on asking me questions about news stories published six and seven years ago.

He put the tissues stained with blood on his desk.

As the red tissues piled up in front of him he concluded the interrogation without having asked me a single question about the coup.

The policemen took me back downstairs. Mehmet was taken up for interrogation.

It was close to midnight.

I sat on the wooden bench and looked at the fuzzy television picture. It was a battle scene, two groups firing at each other. Then a girl and a lad ran away holding hands.

I had not understood from the prosecutor's questions what we would be charged with.

Tired of sitting, I started pacing the cell from one wall to the other.

Two hours later, they brought Mehmet down.

We recommenced waiting.

Then, suddenly, a large group of policemen came and took us upstairs.

The prosecutor had referred us to the court with a request for our arrest.

This was a court with a single judge. The heat made him uncomfortable; he kept fidgeting with the high collars of his robe in an effort to cool himself down.

We had been detained on the charge of "giving subliminal messages," but the allegation had changed quite suddenly. We were now referred to the court for allegedly having participated in the military coup.

When the hearing began, we said to the judge:

"We were detained on the charge of giving subliminal messages, but now that isn't even mentioned. What happened to the 'subliminal message' charge?"

The response the judge gave, a cynical smile creeping over his face, deserves to be recorded in the annals of law:

"Our prosecutors like using words the meanings of which they don't know."

We had languished in a cage in the police lockup for twelve days because the prosecutor *liked using a word the meaning of which he didn't know.* That is what the judge told us.

Then his questions began.

"Couldn't you anticipate that those men would stage a coup?"

Then he added with a self-satisfied smile:

"*I* anticipated it."

Our lawyers objected:

"Failing to anticipate a coup is not a crime. You can't accuse our clients with this allegation."

The judge stretched and said:

"I am not accusing them, dear, we are just chatting."

Then came another odd question:

"You said the government was corrupt?"

The lawyers intervened again:

"The opposition leader also says the government is corrupt . . . Saying the government is corrupt doesn't constitute the crime of putschism."

The judge didn't respond to that.

He turned to me:

"If only you had stuck to writing novels and kept your nose out of political affairs."

We had been taken to court just before dawn on a request that we be sent to prison on charges of "putschism," and the man before us was saying whatever came to mind. I was getting angry:

"You detained us for giving subliminal messages; then you changed the charge without explanation. You alleged that we were putschists. Even if all the judges and prosecutors in this courthouse got together, they wouldn't be able to come up with a single piece of evidence for this."

"I have crusaded against military coups my whole life," Mehmet said, "and now you accuse me of staging a coup because I criticized the government. There is no evidence for this, there can't be."

The judge announced a recess, during which he would make his decision.

It's almost morning, but it's still dark outside.

We are waiting for the judge's ruling.

Will we go home or to prison?

A man asking bizarre questions would decide for us.

We are tired and stressed.

We sit surrounded by a large group of policemen.

I'm looking out the window. The city is quiet. It is asleep. The streets are empty. The streetlights seem dimmed.

Then there is a spurt of activity.

The judge has made his decision.

They take us back to the courtroom.

The judge begins to read the ruling:

"That Ahmet Hüsrev Altan be released under judicial control . . ."

Just as I am about to rejoice I hear the rest of the decision:

"That Mehmet Hasan Altan be sent to prison . . ."

I feel a physical pain. It is as if they've plunged an iron bar through my liver. A sense of rage. A deep sense of despair.

Mehmet turns to me and smiles. He is happy because they are releasing me.

The policemen take us back to the ground floor.

A police car is waiting in the courtyard to take Mehmet to prison.

We hug.

Mehmet tries to console me:

"Don't worry . . . It's good that one of us will be outside."

They put him in the car.

I look beyond it as it leaves.

I realize then that I hadn't said a word to Mehmet as he left.

Two policemen approach me. They will take me from the court and release me.

They push back an iron door and we enter a corridor.

There I see something I've never seen before. Thousands of pink-colored folders have been thrown about on the floor like a bunch of dead turtles. These are files with names, betrayals, murders, separations, bankruptcies and fights stored within them. Lives lost in the depths of a courthouse. A secret cemetery of pink folders.

We make our way through the corridor, kicking and tossing the folders about. There is no end to the corridors, no end to the folders . . . We step on some of them and I feel a sense of unease; it is as if we're stepping on people.

Then the corridors end.

We climb the stairs.

They open the main gate and let me leave.

It is dawn.

The cool morning air gives me a chill.

I take a deep breath.

I am free, angry and deeply sad.

I don't yet know that my sadness will not last very long, that they will issue a "detention order" for me in the evening and I will be arrested.

They will send me to the prison where they have sent my brother.

# Cheating

I get into the police car with four officers from the Anti-Terrorism Branch. They are taking me to the prison.

When the car moves, one of the policemen says, "I read your novel *Cheating*."

I am surprised: "You *did*?"

Among my books, it is the one that received the harshest reviews; provoked the most anger, the most vilification. Despite all this criticism, it sold more than half a million copies.

I don't remember now exactly what it was that critics didn't like in that book in which I told the story of a woman cheating on her husband.

The scene that I remember in relation to that novel is quite different from the story's subject.

I live in a neighborhood where the old Ottoman pashas' mansions with their sprawling grounds have been transformed into large flats with small front gardens in which one can still find bitter orange, pomegranate and plum trees as well as rose beds from the past. The grandchildren of those old pashas still reside in these apartment buildings.

The streets of this neighborhood are quiet and peaceful.

I used to take walks on those streets.

During one of my walks, shortly after *Cheating* had been published, I ran into three ladies chatting just outside a garden.

Three old ladies. One could tell from their simple elegance, from the brooches custom-made for them by jewelers from long ago and whose value only a trained eye would spot, from the single row of pearls around their necks, and from their neatly arranged silver hair and their proud grace that they had spent their youthful years in those mansions.

When they saw me, they turned toward me and blocked my way.

We stood facing one another.

A quizzical, sinful smile was on their faces.

They came closer.

Laughing gently, one of them said:

"How come you know about all that?"

Addressed to a novelist who has told the story of a two-timing woman, this question and the manner in which it was posed amounted to a certain confession, even a partnership in crime.

No charm on earth perhaps is rarer and more provocative than coquettishness wrapped in elegance.

For a few minutes, we savored that confession, then we parted.

I never forgot those ladies.

The question the policemen taking me to the prison asked repeatedly was quite different:

"Do women really cheat like that?"

There wouldn't be many people whose answer to the question "who is more naïve – old ladies from the long-gone mansions or the cops of the Anti-Terrorism Branch?" would be "the cops."

But I can definitely tell you that, when it comes to the subject of women, the police are the more naïve.

# Encounter with Time

One counts everything in prison: the steps one takes round and round the little courtyard; the boiled eggs in the dimpled carton handed through the hole in the door every Tuesday, a whole week's consumption; the cigarettes one smokes throughout the day; the stubborn weeds that grow at the side of the iron spout in the courtyard which lets the rainwater out; the short, sharp calls of the eagle owl that appears around midnight.

A prisoner counts everything. Except time. A prisoner discovers time.

On a warm September day, while a blue cut-glass sky, bright and carefree, watched indifferently what was going on down below, four police officers took me from the courthouse and brought me to a high-security prison sixty miles from the city.

They let me loose into a labyrinth of thick stone walls, dirty yellow in color, and dark brown iron bars. At the entrance to the prison my watch, my books, my cigarettes, my toothbrush – in fact, all my belongings except the clothes I was wearing – were taken away.

They put me in a space resembling the curtained photo booths in shopping malls. I undressed there. They searched all my clothes. They squeezed my shirt collar and sleeves and my trouser hems with their fingernails as if they were checking for lice.

They X-rayed my shoes and my jacket.

Later, as happens in all prison movies, I held my arms out front with my palms facing upward. They put a blanket, a set of blue sheets and a pillow over my arms.

A warden stood by me on either side. We started walking.

We passed by iron bars and iron bars and iron bars along long corridors, turned right and went up the stairs; we passed by iron bars and stopped before an iron door.

The writing on the door said "Ladies Infirmary."

Was putting a male writer, notorious for his fixation on women as subject matter, in a women's sickroom a mere coincidence? Or did the prison administration have a certain sense of humor? I couldn't be sure.

They opened the door and pushed me in, then they closed the door behind me. I heard the iron bolt slip and fit into its sleeve with a deep sound, like fate being sealed.

It was a long hall. There were four undressed iron bedsteads. Stained mattresses had been thrown on the floor. Twelve of them. In the middle stood a white plastic table with an oil stain that was beeswax in color and almost finger-thick.

It was clear that this place had long been used as a storage room.

I took one of the mattresses off the floor and put it on the bedstead near the wall, spread a sheet over it, and placed the blanket and the pillow on top.

Behind the white table, I could see two dark brown doors.

This near black shade of brown was apparently the official color; everything in both the police lockup and the prison was painted with it.

I pushed one of the doors open.

A pitch-black, fidgeting, humming darkness moved behind the door.

I closed it immediately.

It was the bathroom. They had left scraps of food in the bin and the bathroom had filled with thousands of tiny filth flies.

Behind the other door was the toilet.

The barred window of the sickroom looked out to a little stone courtyard.

I lay down on the bed.

Silence. A deep, dark silence. There was neither sound nor movement. Life had suddenly stopped. It did not stir. It was cold and lifeless. Life was dead. It had died suddenly. I was alive, but life was dead.

I used to believe that I would die and life would go on, but life had died and I was left behind.

I had to blow a whiff of air into this dead life. Like God blowing the breath of life into dust to create humankind, I too had to create life from my own breath.

What was the breath that would give life to life? How was I supposed to do this? There was only one way to perform this miracle. To imagine.

As God looking at a pile of clay imagined the complexity we call humankind, I too would look at this dead life, so reminiscent of a pile of clay, and imagine another life.

I would blow my breath.

Like a Bedouin in an endless desert who knows where to find an oasis with plenty of water, I walked confidently toward my inner spring of imagination, the location of which I knew by heart.

Here, I came face-to-face with the terrible truth.

The water had dried, the oasis was gone.

I was not able to imagine. I could not imagine a single thing. My mind was petrified. Not even an image moved inside it. The magical images of the land of my imagination were glued on the walls of my mind like discolored frescos. They were not coming to life.

At that moment, I felt afraid. I was stuck in the corpse of a dead life. I couldn't move, I couldn't get away from it. I didn't have a breath I could blow. I was in the middle of a void; the corpse of life was sucking in all the air around me.

Like Dante entering hell without Virgil at his side, I was slipping down from the circle of "dead life" to a lower circle where the punishment would be harsher.

In that circle, time, which had become heavier and slower with the death of life, was crawling toward me like a gargantuan reptile.

There was no clock making time faster by dividing it into seconds, minutes and hours. There was no movement, no thought, no image dividing time into pieces.

Time had become a single entity: a gargantuan reptile.

When one can't separate the moments, they stick together and become swollen.

They surged and collapsed on me like a translucent mountain of jelly smothering my mind, my soul, my body, filling my mouth and nose, choking me.

*Tempus absoluto.* Absolute time, which Newton said was moving with an uninterrupted speed beyond anything humans could sense, had arrived, gliding in from the universe, and was casting itself over me in this dusty sickroom, leaving me with no room to escape.

Now I understood why human beings invented the clock, why they put clocks on the streets, the squares, the towers.

They did this not in order to know the time; they did it so that they could divide and escape from it.

As the mass of time that had collapsed on me in the midst of that inert, imageless void pressed on my lungs till I thought they might explode, I realized, through intuition more than reason, that I had to invent a new clock.

It took me eighteen steps to walk in zigzags from one end of the sickroom to the other.

If I walked without haste, every step would take a second; if I went back and forth ten times, a total of 180 seconds – in other words, three minutes – would have passed.

I found part of a newspaper page on the floor and tore it into ten small pieces.

At every 180 steps, I put one of those ten pieces on one corner of the table.

When ten pieces gathered at that corner, I calculated that half an hour had passed.

I had invented a newspaper clock.

I had been brought here after having been kept for twelve days in an airless, sunless underground cell at the police headquarters. I was tired. I was exhausted from walking from one corner of the sickroom to the other. But I couldn't stop. For the clock to work, for time to be divided, I had to walk.

I was the clock's coil spring. When I stopped, the clock stopped, and absolute time began collapsing on me.

So I was walking, I was always walking.

The coil spring hurt all over, but I did not stop.

I had managed to divide time into seconds and minutes, but I also wanted to know what hour of the day it was.

In a dusty abandoned sickroom with a bolted iron door, I was fighting with time. I needed every weapon I could muster.

When the sun was at its zenith, the light divided the little stone courtyard, which the sickroom's window faced, exactly down the middle. One half of the courtyard was light, the other half was shady.

Then the light slowly shrank and began climbing the opposite wall.

In my estimation, it reached the top of the wall at around 6 or 6:30 and then retreated for good.

It took the light six hours to travel to the top of the wall from the middle of the courtyard.

I mentally divided the distance between the middle of the courtyard and the top of the wall into six. Now I could estimate what time of the day it was.

I had also invented a solar clock.

In the midst of that dead life, that single piece of void, these were great victories.

I could stop time from advancing slowly, from creeping, from crushing me and exploding my lungs.

For three days, except for the brief periods when I collapsed on the bed in utter exhaustion and fell into a stupor-like sleep, I continuously walked.

I walked. I counted my steps.

At the end of the third day, as I awoke on the bed from a stupor, I felt a miracle stir inside me.

Images were coming back. Scheherazade, who would tell me tales, smiled and ruffled the waves in her hair. The frescos moved.

The oasis began to stir and came back to life.

I had found the divine breath to blow into the dust and give life to life.

I had become the Lord of life and time again.

I had given birth to God.

Five days later they took me out of there. I walked out smiling. I smiled like Moses coming down from the mountain.

Now I live in a cell among thousands of cells. There is a clock in my cell that looks like a green flower with its plastic frame.

I don't sense *tempus absoluto* anymore. It is back in its old place in the universe. No one sees it.

I don't have to count time.

In prison I rediscovered both versions of time – both the unbroken absolute one and the divided one.

Now I have my images and my clock.

When occasionally I return to the prison from my endless excursions into my imagination, I count the eggs, the weeds, the calls of the eagle owl.

Each night, the eagle owl calls three times.

Voyage Around My Cell

When I was eight my views on literature were precise and unshakable and my confidence in myself much greater than it is now.

I had decided O. Henry was the world's best author.

*During Prohibition, the folks who bought one of Andy's two-dollar canes and had the wit to unscrew the head of the cane by two full turns to the right and hold it to their mouth had, as a reward for their acumen, a half pint of smuggled whisky trickle down their throat.*

If the man who wrote this wasn't the world's best author, then who was?

And how about the decision the three grifters made when things got messy, wasn't that wonderful?

*Things had come to such a fine pass that honesty was the best policy.*

One day at a tea garden, I shared my judgment of O. Henry with my uncle's fiancée.

A smile of such kindliness appeared on the young woman's face that, along with the large parasol right behind her, the tablecloth in front of her and the pebblestone pathway on the ground, it became stamped onto my memory like a photograph.

Even at that age I could sense that if someone smiles at you with such kindliness something has to be wrong.

"You might want to wait until you read the classics before making a final decision on that," she told me.

But I wasn't the kind of child who would change his mind for a kindly smile.

I stuck to it.

When I was ten, my father gave me Xavier de Maistre's *Voyage Around My Room.* "You might like this," he said.

I loved it.

O. Henry ceded his throne to this mischievous aristocrat whom the king locked up in his room for dueling, and who described his life and thoughts from within the confines of that room.

To tell of a life from inside a room – now that was something interesting.

I soon discovered there was no such category as "best author."

When they arrested me and threw me in a cell, I inevitably thought about the voyage around a single room.

I too decided to go on a journey.

The cell around which I travel is quite a bit different from de Maistre's.

It has two iron doors; one opens onto the corridor, the other onto the courtyard. The door to the corridor is always locked, but they open the door to the courtyard at 8 a.m. and close it at 6 p.m. every day.

In the middle of the door to the corridor there is a hatch which is bolted from the other side. They serve our meals through that hatch and when they want to say something to us they speak through it. In order to answer, you have to bend halfway down.

The length of the cell is six steps, its width four.

When you enter from the courtyard, there is an antechamber with its own iron door. That is the toilet and shower, with a sink to wash your face and hands. The door doesn't have a lock.

Next to the bathroom a steel sink is mounted on the wall. Our plates, forks, glasses and electric kettle sit there. There is a steel cupboard above. Tea, coffee, sugar, salt, olive oil and the biscuits we buy from the commissary are in there.

Against the wall facing the steel sink is a small fridge, on top of which is a small television.

A stone staircase near the door to the corridor leads to the mezzanine, which has three iron beds secured to the ground by iron nails, and three steel wardrobes. There is no other furniture.

The empty space under the staircase is our storage area, housing a plastic bucket with bottles of detergent in it, a plastic tub in which we wash our laundry, rolls of toilet paper and paper towels, packets of napkins, a case of mineral water, the fan we use in the summer, and extra packages of tea and coffee.

Our small white plastic table is three feet in width and three feet in length, and our three plastic chairs are just to the left of the door to the courtyard.

We spend most of our time sitting in those plastic chairs.

We each bought a thin cushion from the commissary. We aren't allowed to buy a second, so we taped Scotch-

Brite sponges together, placed them in a bin bag and made ourselves extra cushions.

We eat our meals at our plastic table.

I write my defense statements and essays at that table with a ballpoint pen I bought from the commissary.

As I write, my cellmates sit near me and watch TV.

I can write anywhere – sound and movement don't distract me. In fact, once I start writing I stop noticing what's going on around me. I go into an invisible room all by myself and cut off my ties with the rest of the world.

I forget everything that is not part of what I'm writing about.

Forgetting is the greatest source of freedom a person can have. The prison, the cell, the walls, the doors, the locks, the problems and the people – everything and everyone placing limits on my life and telling me "you cannot go beyond" is erased and gone.

The act of writing harbors a magical paradox – it is something that you can take refuge and hide in while at the same time you are opening yourself up to the world and spreading out with your words.

It enables you not only to forget but also to be remembered.

Like all writers, I want both to forget and to be remembered.

The desire to forget is innocent – everyone indulges in it and understands it, and you can easily speak of this desire.

The desire to be remembered isn't tolerated so readily – it's seen as greedy and arrogant, and it makes people angry. People see it as a mortal's claim on a divine right.

So it is.

But what's wrong with wanting to steal the fire that belongs to the gods? Isn't the human adventure also a venture in deification?

Don't we live by becoming continuously both a little more deified and a little more submerged in the banalities of humankind? Doesn't the creative brilliance of our battle against death illuminate the world while, at the same time, we ourselves become tainted in the mire of the pitiful ambitions of beings who forget about death?

Why should we give up on deification?

When one is sentenced to being forgotten on a plastic chair in a cell with its iron door locked from behind, I must confess that the desire to be remembered serves a rather human need for vindication.

As I write, I say, "I will forget you but you will remember me."

How extraordinarily arrogant and self-important, yes.

Still, it is better than insincerity or a hypocritical modesty that asks for people's mercy.

As O. Henry's protagonist said, *Things have come to such a fine pass that honesty is the best policy.*

The plastic table and the chair are for writing and the walks in the courtyard are for dreaming.

Like all people, I have two kinds of dreams. The dreams that can come true and those that can never come true.

The dreams that can come true scare me. I don't know why. I almost never dream about things that can actually happen. But I can't entirely control it and sometimes I do find myself wandering in the land of dreams that can possibly come true. Among such dreams of mine is a house in the country, peaceful and happy. A quiet writing room, a beautiful garden, a creek.

In fact, for someone in my position, no dream can be classified as achievable, but I can't help myself and I still dream that these are achievable dreams.

I escape from them.

I get scared that if I keep dreaming about them they might never come true.

Instead, I throw myself into unachievable dreams. Those are the dreams where I can alter time and space, where I can be in the century and the age of my choosing. It is a magical jungle filled with pleasure and games. There I take life and mold it into a different shape every day.

Sometimes, in between the achievable and unachievable dreams, an image, a voice, a face, a sentence attracts my attention and I immediately take that and put it in a special place in order to nestle it into a novel someday.

Eventually, that single sentence, that single voice, that single image assumes flesh and blood and begins to breed; it becomes a scene from which new people, new voices emerge; it expands like a seed that cracks and germinates; I see people, I listen to them, I talk to them.

I go back to the cell at once and put them down in my notebook.

At such moments, I feel an enormous joy. At such moments, I realize that a corner of my mind that I cannot access is getting ready to write a new novel without even bothering to give me notice.

Indeed, my relationship with that inaccessible corner is quite strange. I know it is there, but I don't try to get in or open its doors; I don't even think of that place. I only wait for all those scenes, all those people I throw in there, to ripen and re-emerge, to tell me at a time I least expect to "go ahead and start writing already."

My walks in the courtyard are filled with ruminations, debates with myself, dreams and scenes of a new novel.

Toward the spring, birds proliferate, they come and sit on the cage above the courtyard.

They coo happily.

During their period of courtship, the male birds bring the females flowers from the fields surrounding the prison – flowers that look like pieces of white lace with the tiniest stems and small daisies in half-bloom.

The birds drop some of these flowers on our courtyard. We take them and put them in an empty soda bottle that we fill with water. We place our bottle-turned-vase in the middle of the table.

The next morning, the wardens come in and take them away. Flowers are forbidden in the prison.

The courtyard has its own seasons, its own suns, its own rains. In the winter, the sun barely grazes the top part of the walls. In the spring, it shines on one corner only. In the summer, the light expands all the way to the center of the courtyard. But in no season is the entire courtyard lit by the sun. There is a side that is always in the shade.

Since I was a child I have thought of the line at which the rain stops, and wondered where that line is.

In prison, I actually saw that line.

It only ever rained on one half of the courtyard. Either the cloud ended in the middle of our courtyard or the walls shielding the wind prevented the raindrops from falling beyond a certain line.

I played with the rain in the courtyard like a child: I took one step and got wet in the rain, I took one step back and stayed dry.

Half of the courtyard was wet, half of it was dry – a strict line separated the two areas. This seemed like a miracle to me. Perhaps it was a miracle.

In my cell, unlike in de Maistre's room, there are no pictures, no trinkets, no sofas, no armchairs. There isn't much furniture here for my mind to mull over in various dreams and thoughts.

I have three stations. I am either in the courtyard, walking or inside, sitting on my chair. Or I am in my bed.

One evening I took a nap and when I woke the moon was shining right above the steel cage, its light covering almost the whole sky. Seeing that silvery light with its dark blue hues gave me a sense of fright. It was dreadful to see something so beautiful in the prison. The moon's light and beauty scared me. Without hesitating, I got out of bed and went downstairs.

Part of me wished to stay and watch the moon, but the other part, afraid of remembering life outside and its beauty, overcame that wish. I escaped from the moon.

Every now and then airplanes go by above the courtyard. I see them from where I lie at night. They travel to free countries. When I see them, I remember the unique smell of the airplane cabins, I remember my own travels, I remember landing in a foreign town and the excitement that makes one tremble inside.

They stir so many aspects of longing all at once that the airplanes also scare me. I don't want to see them.

I live in the same prison as my brother Mehmet Altan, but they keep us in separate cells and don't allow us to stay together. When Mehmet first came to the prison, an inmate who found out from the wardens about his arrival called out to him from an adjacent courtyard, saying, "Mehmet Bey, here you have to forget the outside, otherwise you will have a very difficult time."

This is a piece of sound advice.

You have to forget there is life outside.

But it is not possible to rid yourself of longing. You can forget life but you can't forget people you love, and each beautiful thing you see increases your longing for them.

Sometimes a fit of longing is so acute you feel your lungs cracking, as if a creature inside wants to break out of you. It feels as if you're dying. At such times, you have to move about in order to escape from the creature.

If it's daytime you go out to the courtyard. You walk and walk and walk. For hours. Until you calm down.

But what if it happens at night? You have no place to go, no place to walk, no place to move. You have to sit in a chair. The doors are locked. Those are the hardest hours of the voyage around my cell.

Somehow a strange sense of guilt is mixed in with the sense of longing. You get angry with yourself for "not having told her how passionate you are about her." In fact you have told her, but at that moment it feels like you haven't. You want to tell her at that very moment, but it's not possible. These are the moments when the knowledge that the doors are locked really sinks in.

You remember her face, you remember her voice,

you remember her touch, you remember her smell, you remember her laugh, you remember the things you did together.

It is impossible to describe the kind of longing one experiences in prison. It is so deep, so naked, so primal that no word can be that naked and primal. It is a feeling impossible to describe in words. It can only be described by the growling and moaning sounds of a dog that has been shot.

To understand that feeling, you have to hear the internal laments of prisoners, and you can never hear those.

Those who moan inside can't even let the person they miss so much know; they hide it with embarrassment.

There is a cure for everything. Except longing.

In prison, the lack of resources improves one's creativity. One makes curtains out of bin bags, hanging hooks from teaspoons, dumb-bells from five-liter water bottles, flutes from cardboard, cushions from kitchen sponges, pillow covers from T-shirts.

On the wall near the corridor there is a board for prison notices. We pin pictures there of mimosas and kumquat trees. Flowers of light adorn our board.

The final stop on my journey are the mimosas.

I look at them for a long time.

First I sense their smell, then I hear the rustle of their branches, and the coolness of the wind touches my face.

I find myself by a mimosa tree, moving gently in the breeze.

"Have you come?" a voice says to me. "I've waited for you for so long."

And I look at that mimosa tree. I look at it for days, for weeks, for months.

# The Dream

The last things I see before I fall asleep (on an iron bedstead, under a government-issue blanket) are the bars on the window and the steel cage that is wired across the top of the courtyard.

Yet so far these images have never made it into my dreams. A few times I dreamed about getting out of prison, but I have never dreamed about life here and my experiences in the cell.

I suppose the dream workers inside me are, for the time being, not interested in my prison life.

Once I asked a writer friend of mine who had lived in exile in Sweden for many years in which language he dreamed. The first five years he had dreamed in Turkish, he told me, but after that it was all in Swedish.

Perhaps more time has to elapse for me to have prison dreams.

The dream which made me ruminate on dreams in prison had nothing to do with prison. In fact, it was even too short to be considered a dream.

A woman walked through my dream, a woman I had never seen before. She had an ordinary face, an ordinary body, ordinary clothes. She appeared for a moment and then was gone. I don't remember her face; all I remember is its ordinariness.

The light of the dream barely illuminated the woman. Instead, that mystical light fell on a tiny red spot on the woman's wrist. The only bright thing in the dream was that spot.

I opened my eyes. As I began to stir, the question "what in the world is that red spot?" was already in my mind. I must have begun thinking about it before I awoke.

I was startled.

Like anyone else, I am used to all kinds of dreams.

Each night the unknown quarrymen who begin their work in the depths of our minds once we fall asleep use their mallets to smash into pieces the large blocks of marble that are our thoughts and feelings quarried from life and hewn by our intellect and reason.

Thoughts, desires and fears – all unchained, impossible to fit into any kind of reasoned or intellectual framework, destroying all logical coherence – invade our souls with the weight of their rebelliousness. Like the gods, they create a world that defies all rules.

Dreams are God inside us. Or a madman.

Does this insurrection by the irrational, which is unique to gods and the insane, cater to our being's need for madness, its wish to break free of reason for a while? Or does it deprive us of our reason and keep us in the realm of madness?

I don't know, but I do wonder about the dreams of the insane.

What does a madman see in his dreams?

While sane people go mad in their dreams by experiencing things that have broken free of reason, do the insane come to their senses at night thanks to rational dreams?

The answers to these questions are unknown to me.

People we don't see, know or recognize live in the attics of our houses and at night they move around the belongings we have put in order during the day.

They roam and we don't even know if it is we or they who are the true owners of the place.

We don't control the management of our own houses; dreams are the proof of that.

Each night we are changed by what we see, and each morning we wake up as both ourselves and someone else.

This eerie division of our existence – the harboring inside us of gods and madmen – is a fact that, despite its oddity, we don't find strange anymore; we are used to it, we welcome it as a natural thing.

Like anyone else, I am used to nightmares and happy dreams, I am used to flying, to being scared and to feeling desire.

But a tiny red spot . . . The light falling on that spot only . . . Such a tiny detail being the core of a dream.

I have never met a woman with a red spot on her arm; I don't have a memory or an emotion or a thought that might cause me to dream of a woman with a red spot on her arm.

Until that day, no dreams had stirred such curious, even worrying thoughts in me.

I was appalled by the realization that a tenant, or perhaps a landlord, residing in the depths of my being was capable of conjuring such a tiny detail.

Did someone who could imagine such a spot, who had reason to imagine it, reside inside me without my knowledge?

What kind of details was he interested in?

What had been happening inside me as I lived for the last year and a half in a box made of iron and cement?

Was this red spot the metamorphosis of an impression the outside world had made on me without my noticing? Or was it an image that gave life to itself without any exterior perception?

The impressions the outside world can leave on you are limited in a prison cell. The material for this red spot hadn't come from outside. This bit of ruby was inside me.

Still, this spot had to be made of some raw material.

But which raw material?

All night I surveyed my past, going to the deepest places my memory could reach. I didn't come across a sign or a trace that could show me where that red spot had come from.

Not a sense of longing, not a desire, not a fear, not a certain memory . . . There were no roads in my mind that led there.

I got lost within this tiny spot.

Creating such a minute detail required a more complex imagination than it would take to dream of ghosts, abysses, exaltations, moments of lovemaking; a larger and more inventive imagination.

I sensed a creature hiding in my depths more powerful than I had presumed, and I shivered.

It was as if something had demonstrated its strength to me with a tiny spot.

I lay under the shadows of the iron bars that faded away bit by bit and looked at the ceiling till morning.

The red spot was there.

It flapped like an invader's flag, one that belonged to either a god or a madman.

# Serial Killer

The prison barbershop was next door to the prison tailor.

My turn finally came to go to the barber, and while he was trimming my beard the tailor came in to give the barber a shirt on which he had replaced a missing button.

The second time I went to the barber's, the tailor was sitting there in his white shirt.

I hesitated by the door.

"Come in," said the tailor. "Sit down."

"Aren't you the tailor?"

"When the barber is on leave, I tend his patch."

I sat in the chair.

The tailor shaved my face.

He was a chatty man. "There's nothing we haven't

seen here," he said as he told me stories about the prisoners he had known. I sat and listened on tenterhooks, afraid that he might mistakenly cut my ear or put his scissors up my nose.

He had shaved a serial killer who had been caught after killing four people.

"On visiting days, he used to sit by his mother, knees pressed together like a well-behaved boy."

"Did you ever speak to him?"

"Did I ever!"

"Did you ask him why he had killed those men?"

Of course he had. "How come you killed those men just for your pleasure?" he had asked him.

"What did he say?"

The tailor gave me the killer's answer with a smile on his face.

The answer this well-behaved killer who had cold-bloodedly butchered four people gave to the question *How come you killed those men just for your pleasure?* was far more memorable than the scene in which a tailor shaved an author's face:

He said, "That's just the way it was, then."

# Meryem

There are three of us in the cell: two devoutly religious men and one nonbeliever.

We are together every moment of every day in these cramped conditions.

From completely different families, completely different educational backgrounds, completely different cultures, with completely different habits and completely different tastes, we collide with each other in something resembling a train crash in a thirteen-foot-long cell.

It is not only our culture and beliefs that are different, so too are our ages.

It is as though we had been brought together by a playwright and not by the prison administration, since our identities embody enough conflict and tension to see an entire play through to its climactic end.

Our youngest is thirty-eight years old.

He was born into an extremely pious family. Religion is not merely a set of beliefs for him, it has, since birth, been an indivisible and natural part of his body and soul. I have never seen anyone who wore his faith as simply and comfortably as he does.

He studied cinematic arts. He is familiar with the lifestyle of nonbelievers. Although he has remained in a religious milieu his whole life, he is well aware that people who don't share his beliefs also roam the earth.

He sees prison as an opportunity to cultivate himself and uses that opportunity well. He reads Ibn al-'Arabi and Al-Ghazali as well as Plato, Tolstoy and Murakami.

His family lives far from Istanbul; no one has visited him for a year.

Yet he never complains, because "Everything is God's doing and it is a sin to complain about His deeds." He doesn't commit that sin.

He carries each burden life puts on his shoulders with the same strength and confidence.

He is certain that all problems will be solved by God one day.

The middle member of our family is fifty-three years old. He has been replaced in our cell a few times.

The strange coincidence is that each of these new inmates has been the same age. Their profession, their physical appearance and their place of birth have varied, but when it came to religion they were all the same. Even their dispositions and emotions were exactly the same. They were like a single person who had many disguises.

Sometimes, in the kaleidoscope of my memory, they multiply and assume different faces. At other times, they unify to become a single man. On the subject of religion in particular, my memory doesn't distinguish one from the other.

My mind, like an illusionist, would first show me playing cards with different faces, then shout, "Religion!" and all the cards would turn into the same face.

That "single face" is that of the son of a middle-class family that wasn't overly religious.

His intense relationship with religion began in his youth. He fell in love with religion. His is more than a faith, it is a passion that occupies his entire soul and leaves almost no room for any other kind of emotion or desire.

After adolescence, he spent all his life among people as pious as himself.

Talking about religion gives him an enormous amount of pleasure – no other subject interests him as much.

He spends most of his time reading religious books and performing his devotions.

I am sixty-eight years old.

I don't believe in God but I find the idea of God quite interesting.

We inhabit a planet where living things prey on other living things. Human beings regularly kill not just other creatures but also one another. Fire spurts out of mountains, the earth cracks and devours living creatures, waters run wild and destroy everything in their path and thunderbolts rain down from the heavens.

That humankind can conceive that so dreadful a place was created by a force representing "absolute goodness" and that, despite the violence at the foundations of their being, they still possess such an optimistic imagination seems to me the strangest of human paradoxes.

They believe all this was created by a "force," yet they don't reproach that "force." On the contrary, they worship it with gratitude.

Religion, as the consequence of people's ability to see "goodness" in this terrifying planet of ours, has interested me ever since I was young.

God is a magnificent metaphor.

Like many writers, I enjoy ruminating upon him. The helplessness of human beings, suffocating in their own violence, dreading their own evil, and therefore imagining a focal point of goodness outside themselves as a remedy for their afflictions; this vain effort of theirs seems to me like a sad quest in the human adventure.

First they find a God who tells them to be good and then they kill one another in his name. It sends chills up my spine. What's more, they believe that this very God owns a torture facility called hell.

I suspect that hell takes up more space than heaven in the believers' souls.

In *The Divine Comedy*, Dante's depiction of the Inferno is more intense and dramatic than his narrative on Paradise. Dante cannot help but imagine himself torturing the dwellers of hell. Here are the literary grounds for my suspicion that what we expect from God is not so much that he accept us into his heaven but that he send our enemies to hell.

A God that created Satan and hell . . . Evidently, humankind is unable even to imagine "pure and absolute goodness"!

In spite of it all, that pious search for goodness and

morality arouses in me a reluctant sympathy. The religious look for something to help them be good and moral and resist evil.

But because they think they can only find goodness and morality with the help of God, they can never bring themselves to accept that nonbelievers can also be good and moral people. For them a nonbeliever is in principle amoral and bad. I suppose they accept unwittingly that a person cannot have goodness in himself, that he can become a good person only with outside help.

Our ending up together in the same cell has been quite a baffling experience for all three of us.

Never had I lived with people who prayed so intensely; nor had they ever spent so much time in the presence of a nonbeliever.

Because religion finds the solution to all problems in the afterlife, seeing things through the prism of faith inevitably invokes an image of death.

When my cellmates look through that prism, they see the afterlife, but I only see death.

A loud reciting of the Qur'an, whisperings of prayers, turning off the TV at a certain time all gave me the sense that someone had died. During the first weeks, I lived with the feeling that I would soon see a dead body covered with white sheets in a corner of the cell.

My cellmates, in their turn, were troubled by my gaze – the gaze of an outsider.

Like thorny plants entangled within an iron taw we prickled each other.

We were trying to create some space for ourselves without hurting one another. Our middle one, who had been suddenly extracted from a life of religion and pious people to be confronted with a nonbeliever, could not fathom how a person could still lack faith when presented with the clear and unequivocal facts of God and religion.

He hoped to save me from hell.

For a long time, we talked about religion.

We discussed age-old questions such as why God in his "absolute goodness" created Evil, or who was responsible for a person's deeds.

The middle one was easily offended in matters of religion. Although I knew this, I sometimes couldn't stop myself from teasing him like a teenager.

Then he would be cross and stop talking to me for precisely three days.

Because Prophet Muhammad said, "It is not permissible for a man to forsake his Muslim brother for more than three days . . ." he would make peace at the end of the third day.

But what really angered him was my behavior.

He wanted to lead a pious life, to watch religious discussions on TV.

I, on the other hand, had discovered among the limited number of channels the prison TV offered one that catered to the urban poor, where female singers whom no one had heard of sang and danced in revealing dresses. I liked watching that channel.

He disapproved both of my watching of that channel and of my keeping up a regular exercise regimen.

"You're old," he said to me one day. "You will die soon. Why do you busy yourself with such things?"

"You think I should start performing my devotions because I will die soon?"

"Of course!"

I laughed.

"I am a disciple of Abu Talib," I said.

Abu Talib was the uncle of Prophet Muhammad. He never became a Muslim himself but helped Muslims a great deal.

The first Muslims liked him very much and prayed that he too would accept their faith and go to heaven.

When Abu Talib became ill and took to his bed, they visited and told him this: "You will die soon. Accept Islam and be saved in the afterlife."

"No," said the prophet's uncle, "I won't do anything that will make people say I became a Muslim because I feared death."

It was the middle one who told me this story in the first place.

He laughed when I said, "I am Abu Talib's disciple."

"You will still die," he said, "You are wasting your life away."

Then he brought up that famous theory.

"If you spend the final few years of your life having faith and doing your devotions you will not lose anything. But if you don't believe, you will lose a glorious afterlife. Is it worth it?"

The middle one was very surprised to hear that Pascal was the first to say this.

He took to philosophy.

One evening we were talking about religion again when I told him about Spinoza and then asked: "Does God have any boundaries?"

"May God forgive me," he said, "of course he doesn't."

"Then God embodies everything on earth."

"Of course!"

"Then God's existence doesn't end where my body begins. He embodies me also. Me, you, all of us . . . we are a part of God. Then there is nothing I can call 'I.' Because if I exist separately, there is no God, and if there is God then there isn't a separate me."

He pondered. He would hold back at such instances for he feared saying the wrong thing and committing a sin. "One has to ask religious scholars such a question," he said.

After a while the three of us got used to each other.

It didn't make the middle one so angry that I watched women on TV.

And I had accepted their never-ending acts of devotion as part of life.

On visiting days, the middle one and I went together to the visiting room, where we talked to our families on the phone as they sat on the other side of a thick glass window.

His wife, son and daughter would usually come together to visit him.

His daughter had such a pure, innocent look on her face that my children thought she resembled Mary, mother of Jesus, so we gave her the name "Meryem."

We always referred to the young girl as Meryem.

The middle one went along with this.

After a visit I would ask him, "How is your wife, and how is Meryem?" and without thinking it odd, he would answer, "They're fine."

One day his wife came alone.

After the visit we went back to the cell.

His face was darkened with pain, his shoulders had slumped, and there were tears in his eyes.

"They arrested Meryem," he said.

A moaning sound escaped my lips as if someone had hit me in the stomach with a stick. I saw the face of the youngest of the three of us turn yellow with sadness.

Arresting the twenty-year-old daughter of a prisoner . . . A ruthless hostility that defies all sense of decency.

I could see how grave his heartbreak was, how he burned inside.

"They will release Meryem soon," I said, "and I promise you, when they do that, I will pray with you and give my devotions to God."

He was such a pious man that hearing that a non-believer would bring himself to pray alongside him cheered him up even at his saddest moment.

He smiled.

"Really?"

"Really," I said. "I promise."

He had four very difficult months. He carried his pain with dignity.

After four months, they released Meryem.

Two pious men and a nonbeliever . . . We stood side by side and performed the prayer ritual together.

We thanked God in our cell for Meryem's release.

The Novelist Who Wrote
His Own Destiny

They sit on a bench six-and-a-half feet high, dressed in black robes with red collars.

In a few hours they will decide my destiny.

They don't resemble the Fates who sever the thread of life. With their ties loosened, and with bored expressions, they look more like Gogol's petty public servants.

Their chief, who sits in the middle, splays his right arm across the bench like a piece of wet laundry. He fiddles with his fingers and watches his fingers fiddle.

He has a long, narrow face and plucked, colorless eyebrows. Under swollen half-closed eyelids, his eyes are barely noticeable – they are nothing but a dead wetness.

He has a peculiar tic that becomes more pronounced

143

when the defense speaks: a small node that rolls under his skin all the way from his chin to his eyes.

Every now and then he looks at his mobile phone to read his messages.

When one of the defendants on trial with us says he is about to undergo heart bypass surgery, the chief judge pulls the microphone with its red light toward himself and says in a mechanical voice, "The hospital told us there were no circumstances preventing your stay in prison."

As our defense lawyers speak about the most crucial matters, he again pulls the microphone toward him and says in the same mechanical voice, "You have two minutes, wrap it up."

It is as if the phrases uttered by the defendants and their lawyers strike him on the forehead, break apart and fall to the bench in pieces.

I remember what Elias Canetti said about such people: *Being safe, at peace and in splendor and then to hear a person's pleas while determined to turn a deaf ear . . . Could anything be more vile?*

While the defendants and their lawyers speak, the chubby, skew-eyed judge to the chief's right leans back in his chair and looks up at the ceiling. From the lines of pleasure that move across his face it's clear he is day-dreaming. When he is not daydreaming, he usually leans his head on his hand and sleeps.

The judge on the left busies himself with the computer in front of him, reading continuously.

Toward noon they tell us they will withdraw for deliberations in order, as they say, "to make a decision."

We are surrounded by gendarmerie. At our side is a row of gendarmes, at our back another row. Behind them is another group. They are clad in RoboCop gear with armor-like black stab-vests and kneepads.

A gendarme takes each of us by the arm; we pass between two rows of gendarmes and go down the narrow stairs.

They put us in a tiled holding cell with iron bars at the front.

We are five men.

The sixth defendant, a woman, is separated from us and taken elsewhere.

The Supreme Court, on my brother's appeal, had examined the evidence against us and ruled that "no one could be arrested based on such evidence." This has made the journalists on trial with us optimistic and hopeful.

I am not as optimistic as they are.

We pace the lockup nervously from one end to the other. Our shadows skip over the lines between the tiles and try to catch us.

We feel with a sense of helplessness that we have all but lost our right to determine our own future.

The minutes go by, now faster, now slower, depending on the tempo of our conversations. When the minutes slow down they become razor sharp; we feel bloody cuts opening inside us but we hide them from each other.

*Vulnerant omnes, ultima necat.* "All of them wound; the last one kills." It is a truth known since the ancient Romans. Yet the minutes that creep by in a holding cell while you are waiting to hear whether or not the sentence will be life in prison are more hurtful than all of their siblings.

As the minutes keep wounding me, I realize with some embarrassment that tiny hopes and dreams are meandering beneath my sober pessimism, glittering like diamond dust.

Beneath the strong voice saying, "They are the desperadoes of the law, capable of any sort of criminal act," I hear a whisper saying, "No one can be *that* nonsensical."

I don't turn off that whisper; I become angry with

myself, yet still I refrain from severing my thin link to hope.

Hope is so amiable, so warm and so attractive that no one who is freezing inside can abandon it. Nor does it help knowing that this is an idle, unnecessary weakness.

The pale flickering dreams fed by hope stir shyly in the shadowy folds of my mind: I leave the prison, a deep breath, the first embrace, words of joy, the smell of happiness and a wide sky above . . .

As I daydream about these things, somewhere three men are determining my destiny.

Perhaps they have already made their decision.

Suddenly, the layers of magma in the depths of my memory break with a strong quake, sentences surface like forgotten water flowers that have been floating on a secret underground river.

I remember a passage from my novel *Like a Sword Wound*. This is what I wrote about a character waiting in a room for the verdict after he was arrested:

*The gap between the moment a person's destiny changed and the moment the person realized this seemed to him to be the most tragic and frightening aspect of life. The future became clear, but the person continued to wait for another future with other expectations and dreams without realizing that the future had already been determined. The ignorance during that wait was horrible and to him was humanity's greatest weakness.*

The sentences I remember make me shiver.

I wrote years ago about the turmoil I am going through at this very moment.

I live now what I wrote in my novel.

I am a novelist living his novel.

A sentence resonates within me and makes me shudder with horror, like the chorus in a voodoo mass attended by sorcerers in masks: *My life imitates my novel.*

Years ago, as I was wandering in that unmarked, enigmatic and hazy territory where literature touches life I had met my own destiny but failed to recognize it; I wrote thinking it belonged to someone else.

The destiny I put down in my novel has become mine. I am now under arrest like the hero I created years ago. I await the decision that will determine my future, just as he awaited his. I am unaware of my destiny, which has perhaps already been decided, just as he was unaware of his. I suffer the pathetic torment of profound helplessness, just as he did.

Like a cursed oracle, I foresaw my future years ago, not knowing that it was my own.

The witches of *Macbeth* roam inside me.

How many such witches, sorcerers, oracles reside within a writer?

What else that I wrote will come true?

What other sentences that I no longer remember have I cursed myself with?

I feel I am being dragged into the depths of a vertiginous, wuthering vortex in which novel and life are entangled, where what is real and what is written imitate one another and change places, each disguised as the other.

I am the oracle, the omen and the victim.

With my sentences, I kill the living and resurrect the dead.

Had I unleashed the wrath of the gods because, like all writers, I too have this power? Is that why I have been cursed? Is that why they made me write my own destiny?

Inside this vortex that has me turning and turning I am becoming the hero I created.

What kind of destiny had I chosen for my hero? What sort of ending did he have?

Suddenly, I hear the sound of heavy boots as the gendarmes come running. They line up in two rows. "Come on," says a voice, "the decision has been made."

*The decision has been made.*

At once I remember.

My hero was convicted, that was the destiny I chose for him.

I know now what they have decided for me without hearing the decision.

I too will be convicted because that is what I wrote.

Destiny won't catch me unprepared, for I am the one who determined it.

They take us upstairs. We enter the courtroom and sit down.

The judges come in and put on the black robes they have left on their chairs.

Their chief, the one with dead, wet eyes, reads the decision:

"Life without parole."

We will spend the rest of our lives alone in a cell that is thirteen feet long and ten feet wide. We will be taken out to see the sunlight for only one hour each day.

We will never be pardoned and we will die in prison.

That is the decision.

I am being convicted just like the hero of my novel.

I wrote my own future.

I hold out my hands and they handcuff me.

I will never see the world again; I will never see a sky unframed by the walls of a courtyard.

I am descending to Hades.

I walk into the darkness like a god who wrote his own destiny.

My hero and I disappear into the darkness together.

# The Reckoning

The iron door shut behind me.

We heard the sounds, one after another, of latches, locks and levers.

My cellmates said they were sorry to hear what had happened. They had seen on the news that I had been sentenced to life without parole.

We had talked about it the night before, and deemed the judges mad enough to ignore the Supreme Court's decision and give us the very harshest of sentences.

But it is one thing to wait at the bedside of a terminally ill patient knowing he will die, and another thing to see him die. Even the most hopeless periods of waiting harbor within them a flicker of hope.

Death extinguishes that final flicker. No matter how much you anticipate what will come, when that final hint of a flame goes out, it shakes you to the core.

You realize then that no one can ever be fully prepared for absolute hopelessness.

You remember Saramago's words, *There is no consolation, my sad friend, humans are inconsolable creatures,* and ponder. He must have been talking about the moment when even the final fragment of hope dies away.

It is true that there is no consolation at such moments.

I expected to be sentenced to life in prison, but I still feel the bewildering blow of hope dying away.

At such moments, a person encounters his real face, he sees who he really is.

He understands his need for something other than consolation. Something else, but what?

My cellmates had gone to bed. The lights had been turned off.

I sat in the dark.

The light of the corridor seeped in through the small square peephole slot in the iron door and fell near my feet like a yellow stain. The fierce beam of the searchlight outside reached the courtyard walls, reflecting a phantom light back into the cell, a light that did not illuminate anything but turned everything to transparent shadows.

I lit a cigarette. I looked at its lurid glare in the dark cell.

I could see that my life was about to go down like an old ship in a heavy storm – the cracked boards, creaking hinges, torn sail and wobbling mast all coming to pieces in the waves, to be buried in the watery depths.

I watched my life in the dark. The red glow of my cigarette pulsed like a lighthouse.

I thought: "What will I do? What am I supposed to do?"

I could have cursed the storm and got angry with those who had created it. I could have felt depressed about having fallen right into the eye of the storm. I could have complained about my fate.

None of that would calm the storm.

Indeed, I wasn't supposed to be thinking about the storm.

Like Odysseus facing Poseidon's fury, I had to use all my strength to survive, and for that I had to focus not on the storm but on what was within my capacity. I had to write my own Odyssey in this dark cell.

To save oneself from the monstrous waves, the sirens and the man-eating Cyclopses, one must resist and fight.

There was the storm and there was me.

We were going to fight.

Oddly, the vastness of the storm increased my desire to defeat it. The blows that obliterated all hope strengthened my instinct to cling more tightly to that hope.

My ship could crack, break and sink but I would keep fighting to the end.

I would prepare myself for the worst but I wouldn't stop hoping for the best. I wouldn't give in to fatigue and depression. I would never forget that my dream of reuniting with my Penelope could someday come true.

I lit another cigarette. The lurid glare glowed again.

I must confess that even from within a dark cell, the idea of fighting filled me with such exuberance that I was saying, "To the end," with excitement.

I liked fighting more than I liked consolation.

Even though they had sentenced me to death in a cell I wasn't dead yet. The last glimmer of hope was still there.

The decision to fight made the glimmer more alive.

A love of fighting was in my blood.

My great-grandfather's nickname in the army was "Mad Hasan Pasha." Legend has it that he truly deserved his moniker. He trained as an artilleryman in Germany, fought in the Balkan Wars, assumed the role of front artillery commander in Gallipoli and was in the Turkish Liberation War from beginning to end. He spent ten years of his life fighting one battle after another.

My great-grandfather was sentenced to death for helping rebels to defect to Anatolia during the War of Liberation. He escaped being hanged at the last minute.

My father was put on trial hundreds of times for his writing; he was in prison for years.

My brother is sentenced to life in prison.

But in my own personal Odyssey there is yet another trait that underlies this adventurous inheritance and gives it a tragic touch of irony. For my love of fighting conflicts with my fondness for comfort; I enjoy worldly pleasures, know we only live once and don't have much regard for heroism and bravery.

Indeed, I find bravery disgraceful in a writer.

A writer should be admired and praised for his writing alone. He should place himself before his readers bare of all but his writing. He should never entertain or deceive his readers by putting on shows of bravery.

At the conclusion of Arthur Miller's *The Crucible*, a play I watched at a very young age, the protagonist has to sign a document to save his life and, at first, he refuses.

Later he says to himself, *If I don't sign, they'll think I am a brave person; I will have deceived people.*

There are times that others think I am a brave person, and when that happens I feel embarrassed. "I have been deceiving people," I think to myself.

I am not a brave person.

I am a person who likes being brave but, at the same time, I scorn bravery. I am the very embodiment of a contradiction.

Besides, a question that deepens this contradiction further has occupied my mind since my youth: which is more important, the writing or the writer?

What becomes a writer more – protecting his honor or giving up his honor for the sake of his writing?

Should he protect his honor by fighting, resisting, struggling while, in turn, limiting the space he can give to his writing?

Or should he give up his honor and the chance of helping the people who might need his pen, in order to dedicate his whole life to writing?

In this duel, I chose to protect my honor and, as a result, I feel a strange sense of shame.

"I should have been brave enough to choose the writing over the writer, but I didn't have the courage," I say.

I torment myself: "You chose the writer," I say. "If you were a good writer, you would have chosen the writing."

Then, in an effort to protect myself, I say: "I have to like the writer too. If I don't like myself, how can I have the confidence to write?"

And then there is the woman I love, of course. I shouldn't embarrass her.

That famous story comes to my mind – the one I heard many times when I was a child and then wrote about many times:

Paetus, a Roman commander, rebelled against the emperor, but was caught and sentenced to death.

Since in ancient Rome "ordinary people" were forbidden to touch a noble, members of nobility who were sentenced to death would be left alone in a room with a knife.

Paetus entered the room.

His mother, father, siblings and wife waited outside the door to hear his dead body fall on the floor.

From inside they could hear Paetus' footsteps. He couldn't bring himself to end his life.

His wife couldn't stand this, so she opened the door and went in, took the knife and plunged it into her stomach, then took it out and gave it to her husband:

*Non dolet, Paete.*

"See, Paetus, it doesn't hurt."

So, what was I supposed to do? Should I have embarrassed the woman I love just so that I could write in comfort? Should I have turned my back on the people who needed me?

There is no easy answer to these questions.

On the one hand, you enjoy fighting and aspire to be your own hero. You were raised admiring brave souls and dread the idea of embarrassing people who love you. You cannot bear the idea of acting like Paetus. Yet you also believe bravery is an unbecoming trapping for a writer, and find it shameful to protect the writer rather than the writing. The wounds this conflict opens will never heal.

There is only one way then for your bravery to be pardoned: by struggling in the middle of the storm but at the same time continuing to write.

By snatching pages – albeit tainted by bravery – from the hands of time as they pass through this cell . . .

The red glow pulsates.

All night I hear the sirens of the police cars bringing new inmates to the prison.

I am in the center of a storm.

I will fight. I will be brave and I will despise myself for it. I will be injured by my inner conflicts.

I will write my own Odyssey, write it with my life in this narrowest of cells.

Like Odysseus, I will act with heroism and cowardice, with honesty and craftiness, I will know defeat and victory, my adventure will end only in death.

I will have the Penelope of my dreams.

I will write in order to be able to live, to endure, to fight, to like myself and to forgive my own failings.

The searchlight sweeps the courtyard. A ghostly glow reflects off its walls and seeps in.

A ship stands in the middle of the cell; its timbers are creaking. On its deck is a conflicted Odysseus.

What a beautiful scene to describe.

I reach for a pen with a hand that is white in the ghostly light.

I can write even in the dark.

I take the ship cracking in the storm in the palm of my hand and begin writing:

*The iron door shut behind me . . .*

The Judge's Concern

Rather bizarre things are happening to me.

A court sentenced me to life without parole on the charge that I am a "religious putschist," putting forward only three of my columns and a television appearance as what they call evidence.

Ten days later, the same court put me on trial again, this time on the charge that I am a "Marxist terrorist," basing its claim on the same column that had allegedly proved I was a religious putschist.

The same court, the same column, two diametrically opposed accusations.

In the second trial (in which I was accused of being a

"Marxist terrorist"), the chief judge continually interrupted my lawyers' defense and told them to "cut it short."

At the end, the judges said they would rule and turned off their microphones.

The three of them talked among themselves for two or three minutes.

As they were about to finish their conversation, the microphones were somehow turned back on and the last sentence spoken by the presiding judge was heard aloud in the courtroom:

"My gosh, we will miss the five o'clock!"

He was worried they would miss the service bus, which would leave at five.

Then he read the verdict against me:

"Six years in prison."

Within three minutes, I had been sentenced to six years, and the judges had missed the service bus.

We were both upset, but I think the judge was more upset than me.

# Wood Sprites

For months, I didn't see a single book, I didn't touch one.

It was forbidden to have books delivered from "outside." The prison had a library, but for whatever reason it was closed.

I grew up in a house full of books. My childhood was spent among them. Books were the wood sprites in a forest the essence of which I couldn't quite grasp, one that looked quite complex and boring to me. I liked the fairies' bright charm, their air of mystery, their promising smiles more than the forest itself.

The first time I went missing I was five years old. After searching for hours, my parents found me in a bookstore that had recently opened in our neighborhood. I was sitting on the floor between two bookcases with a pile of books in front of me.

The small runes on the paper came alive and gleamed as soon as you laid eyes on them; they metamorphosed from one shape to another, transforming themselves into unknown cities, narrow streets, steep rocks, deserts and palaces. They sprinkled you with drops of magic water and you too were transformed. You became Peter Pan, you became Le Chevalier de Pardaillan, you became Arsène Lupin, you became Sherlock Holmes, you became Ivanhoe, you became Lancelot.

I spent the years of my childhood playing with the wood sprites. I got used to having them always around me as they slept in between pages, ready to wake and start dancing as soon as I opened a book. I loved watching them even in their sleep.

One of the things I found most difficult in prison was to live in a place where there were no books.

Finally, they gave us a list of the books in the library. The list resembled a junkyard with a few jewels strewn here and there. There were many useless books but there were also books you'd never have guessed you would find in a prison.

Everything is done by petition in prison, so I immediately wrote asking to be given the books I wanted.

I didn't hear back for a long time.

Just as I was about to give up hope, the hatch in the middle of the door opened one morning and a book fell through.

I took the book from the floor with the ecstasy of a mariner shouting, "Land ahoy!" after sailing the open seas for many months without hope.

I was reunited with the wood sprites, they who gave me such immense joy, boundless confidence and an excitement that sent shivers through my body.

It was as if life had suddenly changed; a crack from the inner depths set a continent adrift.

I wasn't helpless, I wasn't alone, I wasn't lost.

I had a book in my hands.

They had given me Tolstoy's *The Cossacks*.

Tolstoy, that conflicted Zeus of literature, had come to our cell.

In the most unexpected of places, I had happened on a book by a genius, one who can describe an infantry sergeant as elegantly as he would a princess; one who, in Virginia Woolf's words, "reveals the most carefully hidden secrets of human nature" and is "able to read the minds of different people as certainly as we count the buttons on their coats."*

It made me especially happy that the first guest in my cell was Tolstoy because this man, whom Woolf held up as an example to all writers, had been my guide to deciphering the secrets not only of people but of literature itself. Ever since I first read Tolstoy, I have sounded the depths of every statement regarding literature and writers by holding it against his image. Many a phrase and many a claim have lost their luster and dimmed in his shadow.

Tolstoy's shadow was as great as his light, a shadow cast on eras beyond his own.

Tolstoy could capture and hold life in the palm of his hand as easily as a farmboy catches a ladybird. His majestic shadow falls on twentieth-century literature.

All the great writers of the nineteenth century intimidated the writers of the twentieth, but I think the most intimidating was Tolstoy.

Like travelers seeking an alternative route around a mountain range they believe too steep to climb, writers of the twentieth century looked for other paths so they

---

*Translator's note: This quote is taken from the *Times Literary Supplement* (https://www.the-tls.co.uk/articles/public/unsurpassable-tolstoy/).

would not be compared with Tolstoy. Very few writers dare hold life in their palms in order to reshape it.

While nineteenth-century literature told us about people's emotions in staggering depth and revealed the most carefully hidden secrets of human nature, the literature of the twentieth century veered toward ideas.

It veered toward ideas because writing about ideas is always easier than recounting emotions and reading people's minds.

Ideas in a novel contain grave dangers, because ideas represent the author in the novel. The more ideas there are, the more present is the author. The more present the author, the more constricted the space for characters. They cannot develop and, more importantly, they cannot gain depth.

When you look at the great classics of the nineteenth century, you see that characters come before the writer. Le Père Goriot comes before Balzac, Anna Karenina supersedes Tolstoy, Madame Bovary supersedes Flaubert, the brothers Karamazov supersede Dostoyevsky. The opposite is true in the twentieth century, where writers come before their characters.

If you look at *The Man without Qualities* by Robert Musil, one of the most extraordinary writers in the history of literature and one who attached such importance to ideas that he said he wanted to write an autobiography of ideas, you will see that Musil takes precedence over Ulrich. The book is not Ulrich's book, it is Musil's book.

Similarly, Céline comes before Bardamu, Joyce before Bloom.

The major difference between the novels of these two centuries lies, I think, in the importance of the ideas and the writer within the novel.

I like to read novels in which characters' emotions and relationships have the upper hand.

In novels, I prefer the complexity of emotions to the clarity of ideas; my beloved wood sprites become vivid with emotions, but pale when ideas dominate the text.

I believe ideas should not give birth to the novel, but that the novel should give birth to ideas.

Of course, literature is not a prescription of exact formulas, and those who assert the very opposite of what I am saying here and now, and with much more authority, may prefer another color of literature's rainbow.

At the end of the day, we all write what we can, and *then* develop notions of why novels have to be written the way we write them.

Tolstoy wrote about people's emotions because he could read people's minds and write about how they felt.

He managed this with a miraculous sense of intuition.

I don't know how anything but "intuition" could explain how this man who knew nothing of female sexuality was able to write *Anna Karenina*.

Tolstoy believed women didn't enjoy lovemaking. Doris Lessing thought this critical delusion could be explained by the manner in which Tolstoy made love to his wife: he attacked her like a lustful bear, and when she turned him down he thought all women disliked having sex.

Yet this lustful bear created some of the most unforgettable female characters in literature.

I doubt there's another example that can better prove that genius in literature is a result of intuition rather than ideas and knowledge.

I know that contemporary Western literature hugely underrates intuition, even to the point of treating it as "kitsch." But when I look at Balzac, Tolstoy and Dostoyevsky I cannot help but think that if they had written their novels using only their ideas and not their intuition no one would remember them today.

Taking my argument to extremes – using the infinite liberty of a man in a prison cell with no one else to debate or discuss with, no one on whom to try out his ideas – I will even go so far as to say this:

A novelist is helped not only by his intuition, but also by a certain amount of ignorance when he is giving depth to his novel.

It is perfectly possible that I am arguing this in an attempt to have my own ignorance tolerated; nonetheless, I haven't given up my belief in the importance of ignorance to literature.

A novelist keeps the knowledge he truly needs deep down in his mind, in a secret repository not far from where his intuition resides – a repository so well hidden that even the novelist himself doesn't know what has been accumulating there.

In order to access this hidden intuition when writing, the novelist cracks his own mind as if breaking the hard shell of an exotic fruit with the sweep of a heavy broadsword to reach the nectar at its core. He must dismantle his own being in order to reach the bedrock and attain the secret knowledge that will astonish even himself.

Once he strikes this blow against himself, the more the broadsword chafes against the ideas and information accumulated on the surface, the more difficult it will be to reach the nectar.

Surface knowledge is not much use to the novelist. He needs the truths that have seeped through life to the very bottom. With the knowledge that astonishes even himself, he writes his novel.

Flaubert said, "Madame Bovary, *c'est moi*" for a reason. He came across Emma Bovary's emotions not on the surface but in that deep-down repository. There was the knowledge he had accumulated unwittingly.

There is something animal-like in writing a novel, something that relies purely on instinct and intuition. It is indeed why that "ignorant and lustful bear" could write *Anna Karenina*; he could arrive at such precision only by way of a primal beastliness.

The first book that I managed to get my hands on after months without drove me crazy. I pressed the book against my chest and paced up and down the courtyard, sensing the ideas rushing into my mind and colliding with one another.

I savored the joy of possessing a book.

Only after I had calmed down a bit did I come in, sit on a plastic chair and begin to read.

The young Olenin, bored with the superficiality of

Moscow, he who is so full of admiration for the natural ways of the Cossacks; the beautiful Maryanka who sits on her bed and watches with indifference as life goes by; the selfish Daddy Eroshka; the peasants who take pride in stealing; Tatars and Cossacks killing each other just for fun; jugs full of wine drunk with a cup of honey, the gardens separated by wooden fences, the scents of herbs and flowers, the neighing horses, the crowing roosters, romances, battles, the sounds of gunshot . . .

Truth be told, this is one of the weakest of Tolstoy's books. The young Tolstoy was so eager to tell his readers about the different culture and the different nature he had encountered that he wrote the novel from the pieces of knowledge that sit on the surface, and in this loosely woven book the writer takes precedence over his protagonist.

The book had become not Olenin's but Tolstoy's book.

The novel was the victim of an excess of knowledge.

Like Pushkin in *The Captain's Daughter*, Tolstoy had fallen into the trap of facts and pushed his plot and characters to the background in order to relate more of what he had seen.

Young Tolstoy's ideas and knowledge had shaped the novel, not his intuitions.

I saw all that, but frankly I didn't care.

I surrendered myself to the alluring mystery of the wood sprites who took me to riversides and village gardens, to battlegrounds and innocent love affairs, all the while dancing on the gleaming sentences and vivid descriptions scattered here and there in the text that foretold Tolstoy's brilliant future.

I was reunited with books and with my sprites.

The forest had once again become a place of joy.

# The Notice

In prison, you worry about the people you love. How are they doing on the outside, are they all right, how is their health, do they have enough money? All sorts of questions run through your mind.

News from the outside reaches you only after it has undergone several transformations and traveled through the narrowest of channels, like the tapered glass piping in a chemistry lab.

Your visitors keep things from you if they think you will be sad to hear them. You draw conclusions from their voices, their gazes, their unfinished sentences and the half-truths they let slip without meaning to.

One day, I saw an obituary notice in the newspaper.

My uncle-in-law had died. I felt a chill through my spine.

I had known my uncle-in-law since childhood. We had been neighbors in the same building for thirty-five years and he was the doctor to whom I would take my problems before seeing anyone else. Now he was gone from this world.

Because they thought I would be sad to learn this, they kept it from me.

I didn't tell them that I had found out about his passing because I thought they would be sad to think the news had made me sad.

My uncle-in-law is still alive in those slender communication channels I have with the outside.

He will live on until I get out of prison.

I will bid him farewell when I am out.

Until then, we keep him alive through our mutual silence.

# Handcuffs

With each movement of your arms the iron handcuffs tighten. That's how the mechanism works. Even if the gendarme doesn't make them tight as he cuffs you, after a while the iron rings begin rubbing into your flesh. They leave red marks on your wrists. It hurts.

When you walk handcuffed, you realize you don't only need your legs to walk, you also need your arms. It is difficult to keep your balance without moving your arms. You move them unavoidably when you walk. This tightens the cuffs.

On the morning I was taken to hospital for an X-ray, the gendarme handcuffed me. Three other inmates came along.

They put all four of us on the prison's transit vehicle. Because we had a hard time climbing into the bus with our hands cuffed together, the gendarmes held our elbows and pushed us up.

They had built iron cells in the bus. They were five feet long and five feet wide. In each cell there were two rows of iron chairs, three at the front and three at the back. The chairs didn't move, they were secured to the floor.

The only window was at the top of the cell, a hand span across, with thick glass and iron bars. You couldn't see outside.

They made the inmates sit in the iron chairs, side by side. Our shoulders brushed against one another.

Then they pulled the iron door shut and locked it.

If there was an accident, no one could rescue us.

A few years ago, one of these buses had turned over and caught fire and the handcuffed inmates locked inside the cells burned to death.

Perhaps because we knew about this incident we all felt, as the door was being locked from the outside, as if we were being shut into an iron coffin.

The bus moved. It was a bumpy ride. At each bump

the handcuffs tightened a bit more. Our shoulders kept hitting each other.

The three men coming to the hospital with me were all former judges going to see a psychiatrist. They were around forty to forty-five years of age.

We started talking.

They had been arrested in various cities on the charge that they had participated in the military coup.

One of them spoke:

"There is nothing in my file, no evidence whatsoever. The judge who arrested me was my close colleague. We worked side by side. After he ordered my arrest, he hugged me and sobbed. 'If I hadn't arrested you, they would have arrested me,' he said."

They couldn't fathom what had brought this disaster upon them. They themselves had arrested hundreds, perhaps even thousands, of people during their careers. It had never occurred to them that a similar fate might befall them someday.

The judge who was sitting in front of me turned around.

"I didn't know the prison was such a place." He stopped for a moment, then added, "In fact, I never thought what kind of a place prison was."

The one near me spoke with almost childlike naiveté: "I wouldn't have arrested so many men had I known prison was like this."

They spoke with a surprising degree of candor. They had been struck by a disaster they had thought only happened to others, certainly never to themselves, and so were totally unprepared and devastated when it came.

I saw that those who had great power and impunity were less resilient when faced with the jarring blows of life. Now that they had been cast from the pinnacle on which they had once ruled over other people's destinies, they suffered more than the rest as they hit the ground. The severity of the impact shattered their souls.

They told me that the inmates who went to see the psychiatrists most often were the former prosecutors and judges.

One of them was leaning his head against the iron door. He was almost in tears:

"I can't take this place any longer. I miss my family."

His pain was so grave that it drained all his energy, and he lacked the strength to hide it. Then, perhaps, he didn't want to hide his pain. In fact, he wished only to talk of it, nothing else mattered to him. It was as if all that was left of him was the pain he felt. Like a person waving furiously to shake off something stuck to his hand, he was shaking his very being to free himself from the pain affixed to his consciousness.

I was afraid he would begin sobbing.

At that moment, the bus stopped. We had arrived at the hospital.

They opened the cell door.

We got down off the bus, taking careful steps so as not to lose our balance. By now the handcuffs had begun squeezing my wrists.

A gendarme took me by the arm.

The judges were escorted to the psychiatrist. The gendarme and I went to the X-ray department. We waited in the corridor for our turn.

A hospital worker passed by and said, "Get well soon, Ahmet Bey," almost without moving his lips. A friendly voice. I smiled only slightly so the others wouldn't notice.

When it was our turn, we went into the X-ray room.

The gendarme held my wrists ready to remove the handcuffs. Then we heard a voice:

"There is no need for the handcuffs to be removed."

I turned to look. It was a petite young woman wearing a headscarf, loose clothes and no makeup. She was the X-ray technician.

She knew the handcuffs were hurting my wrists and making it difficult for me to move, yet with a voice like ice she stopped their removal.

There was no anger, no irritation, no sign of enmity on her face.

Neither was there compassion, grace or mercy.

Her face was dispassionate, as empty as a frame.

She had eyes, eyebrows, a mouth, a nose and a chin, but no expression.

I had never seen such an impassive face before, it had no trace of emotion.

Here was pure evil neither nurtured by nor derived from or mingled with any kind of emotion. She was evil just to be evil and you couldn't even tell whether she took pleasure in it or not.

She wanted the old man who was standing before her with his white beard to suffer even more, the handcuffs digging ever deeper into his skin.

This young woman's faith was strong. She expressed her devotion in her manner and her attire. Presumably she never skipped a prayer and performed her devotions five times a day. She pleaded with God to "guide us to the straight path" each time she prayed.

The holy book of her faith said: *amr bil ma'rouf wa nahi anil-munkar.*

God commanded his servants to *do what is right and prevent what is wrong.* The Qur'an emphasizes that people were created to do good. The Prophet Muhammad teaches that heaven belongs to the merciful.

This young woman knew all this. She clearly wished to go to heaven, but she acted from malice and not mercy. Why? Did she think what she was doing wasn't evil?

Yet that wasn't possible.

This X-ray technician would have described it as "heartless and evil" if an irreligious young woman had treated an imam of my age the same way she was treating me.

So why, then, did this young woman commit evil despite the clear commands of her faith?

Clearly she did not see me as a human being; for a reason unknown to me she had cast me out of her circle of good and evil.

Concepts like sin and merit, goodness, evil and morality did not apply to me. She felt no need to treat me with kindness or consideration.

I was a nothing for her, a nonexistence, and far beyond the reach of religion or ethics.

It was as if in that young woman's mind a curtain invisible to me had been drawn tight around religion, ethics, intelligence and emotion, outside of which was a vast emptiness reserved for handcuffed people like me.

Evil occupied that emptiness.

I had no doubt that outside the prison hospital this young woman behaved as a pious, moral and compassionate person. Those values were not all gone, but the space they occupied was greatly reduced.

With handcuffs around my wrists, I stood before the X-ray machine. She told me how I had to stand in an expressionless voice.

As she X-rayed me I thought about her.

Like anyone, I am accustomed to evil. But I have found that sometimes anger, sometimes wit and sometimes even kindness can be added to evil, or sometimes revenge or an anxiety to reap the rewards of a situation. An evil that stood alone in such emptiness struck me as a travesty lacking anything inherently human.

She X-rayed me, and then she recorded my data in her book with the same expressionless face.

The gendarme and I left the hospital and got onto the bus.

The judges came too.

Again, they put us in the iron coffin and locked the door.

The judges' "therapy" had been shorter than I expected.

"What happened?" I asked.

The psychiatrist they saw didn't let them have their handcuffs removed, either. The judges, suffering from the psychological trauma of being incarcerated and handcuffed, described their affliction to the "doctor" with handcuffs around their wrists.

A psychiatrist who treats his patients without having their handcuffs removed.

This baffled me even more than the X-ray technician.

"Are all consultations with patients at the prison hospital conducted with handcuffs? Is this the rule?" I asked.

"Not at all," the judges answered. "It depends on the doctor. Some have them removed and some, like the psychiatrist today, have them left on."

Piety without mercy, doctoring that makes a sick patient worse: the treatment we received did not fit well with the standards of either religion or medicine.

There must have been an explanation for the similarities between the attitudes of the X-ray technician and the psychiatrist. Was it working in a prison hospital that made them so callous and caused them to forfeit all decency?

But the man who wished me well and the previous doctor who had the judges' handcuffs removed also worked at the prison hospital.

Not everyone behaved the same – the effects of the prison hospital were different on different people.

I recalled the strikingly simple finding by Viktor Frankl, the man who endured much suffering as a prisoner in Auschwitz and who later founded the logotherapy method of psychiatry. After observing the different reactions of the prisoners and guards at the camp, he concluded that *some people were noble and some were ignoble. There might be ignoble ones among the prisoners and there might be noble ones among the guards.*

The doctor, who dedicated his whole life to seeking a remedy for the turmoil of a human soul, arrived at this judgment after having been subject to gruesome cruelty – a judgment which, when I first read his book, took me by surprise.

Could the attitudes we encountered have such a simple explanation?

There was doubtless an element of truth in the words

of this scientist whose knowledge and experience of pain went far beyond my own.

It seems that, given the right climate, ignobility is able to grow and flourish, regardless of how it is dressed up. Such people let their ignobility emerge when they find the opportunity and power to do evil.

Of course, this kind of ignobility is not punished, but rewarded. No one would get angry because they treated us that way; perhaps they would even be given a pat on the back.

When the bus bumped and lurched around a curve my back slammed against the iron chair and the impact made me raise my hands in the hope of holding on to something. This made the handcuffs tighten even further around my wrists.

Suddenly, I realized that what I had been feeling was all wrong. I should have been angry, furious or even sad. Instead, I had forgotten about those feelings and, like a botanist coming across a new species of plant, had busied myself examining those whose behavior went against their religious beliefs and professional ethics.

I suppose this was my defense mechanism. I didn't feel an emotional attachment to the petty acts of evil and humiliation I encountered. Instead, I classified each attitude and tried to understand the reasons behind it so that I could store it in the drawers of my memory, to take it out and write about it someday.

This method served its purpose.

Although not quite conscious of having made such a choice, I had succeeded in building an invisible wall to protect myself against all that was happening.

When they treated you like you were nothing, you could counter it by acting as if they were a topic of research.

The bus stopped and we got off.

At the prison entrance they removed our handcuffs.

My wrists had purple bruises around them.

I had set out to get better, but had come back scarred by evil.

I did not go to the hospital again.

The Bird

Each cell in the prison has a stone courtyard in front that is six steps long and four steps wide, with an iron drain in the middle for the rainwater to flow away.

The high walls of the courtyard have barbed wire on them. A steel cage covers the top.

To use the title of the novel my father wrote in prison, "a handful of sky" is what you see when you look up, but even that is divided into the small squares of the steel cage above.

When spring arrives, birds of passage fly in through the cage and make nests on the barbed wire.

The inmates pacing in their adjacent courtyards

don't see each other but they can talk by shouting. We recognize one another from our voices.

On occasion, my young cellmate Selman chats with our neighbors whom we don't know.

What they talk about doesn't matter.

What matters is knowing there are people present beyond your cell walls and letting them know of your existence.

For us, the world is the neighboring courtyards that our voices can reach. Shouting is our way of communicating with the world.

One spring day, Selman was talking to the voice in the courtyard next to ours.

"The birds have started migrating here," Selman said.

"I am looking after a parakeet," the voice answered. "He was born in the prison, then his mama died and I raised him."

"I've never seen your parakeet flying about," said Selman. "I guess I am never there at the right time."

"He doesn't fly," said the voice in the next courtyard.

Then, with the compassion of a father feeling sorrow for a child, the voice added:

"He is afraid of the sky."

The Writer's Paradox

*A moving object is neither where it is nor where it is not,* concludes Zeno in his famous paradox. Ever since my youth I have believed this paradox better suited to literature or, indeed, to writers than to physics.

I write these words from a prison cell.

Add the sentence "I write these words from a prison cell" to any narrative and you will add tension and vitality, a frightening voice that reaches out from a dark and mysterious world, the brave stance of the plucky underdog and an ill-concealed call for mercy.

It is a dangerous sentence that can be used to exploit people's feelings, and writers do not always refrain from using such sentences in a manner that serves their interests when the possibility of touching a person's feelings is at stake. Even understanding that this is their intention may be enough for the reader to feel compassion toward the writer of that sentence.

Wait. Before you start playing the drums of mercy for me, listen to what I tell you.

Yes, I am being held in a high-security prison in the middle of a wilderness.

Yes, I am in a cell where the door is opened and closed with the rattle and clatter of iron.

Yes, they give me my meals through a hatch in the middle of that door.

Yes, even the top of the small stone-paved courtyard where I pace up and down is covered with a steel cage.

Yes, I am not allowed to see anyone other than my lawyers and my children.

Yes, I am forbidden from sending even a two-line letter to my loved ones.

Yes, whenever I must go to the hospital they pull handcuffs from a cluster of iron and put them around my wrists.

Yes, each time they take me out of my cell, orders such as "Raise your arms, take off your shoes" slap me in the face.

All of this is true, but it is not the whole truth.

On summer mornings, when the first rays of the sun come through the naked window bars and pierce my pillow like shining spears, I hear the playful songs of the birds of passage that have nested under the courtyard eaves, and the strange crackles prisoners pacing other courtyards make as they crush empty water bottles under their feet.

I wake up with the feeling that I still reside in that pavilion with a garden where I spent my childhood or, for whatever reason (and I really don't know the reason for this), at one of those hotels on the cheery French streets of the film *Irma la Douce*.

When I wake up with the autumn rain hitting the window bars, bearing the fury of northern winds, I start the day on the shores of the Danube River in a hotel with burning torches out front, which are lit every night. When I wake up with the whisper of the snow piling up inside the window bars in winter, I start the day in that dacha with a front window where Doctor Zhivago took refuge.

I have never woken up in prison – not once.

At night, my adventures are filled with even greater activity. I wander the islands of Thailand, the hotels of London, the streets of Amsterdam, the secret labyrinths of Paris, the seaside restaurants of Istanbul, the small parks hidden in between the avenues of New York, the fjords of Norway, the small towns of Alaska with their roads snowed under.

You can run into me along the rivers of the Amazon, on the shores of Mexico, on the savannahs of Africa. I talk all day with people who are seen and heard by no one, people who don't exist and won't exist until the day I first mention them. I listen as they converse among themselves. I live their loves, their adventures, their hopes, worries and joys. I sometimes chuckle as I pace the courtyard, because I overhear their entertaining conversations. As I don't want to put them on paper in prison, I inscribe all of this into the crannies of my mind with the dark ink of memory.

I know that I am a schizophrenic as long as these people remain in my head. I also know that I am a writer when these people find themselves in sentences on the pages of my books. I take pleasure in swinging back and forth between schizophrenia and authorship. I soar like smoke and leave the prison with those people who exist in my mind. Others may have the power to imprison me, but no one has the power to keep me in prison.

I am a writer.

I am neither where I am nor where I am not.

Wherever you lock me up I will travel the world with the wings of my infinite mind.

Besides, I have friends all around the world who help me travel, most of whom I have never met.

Each eye that reads what I have written, each voice that repeats my name holds my hand like a little cloud and flies me over the lowlands, the springs, the forests, the seas, the towns and their streets. They host me quietly in their houses, in their halls, in their rooms.

I travel the whole world in a prison cell.

As you may well have guessed, I possess a godly arrogance – one that is not often acknowledged, but that is unique to writers and has been handed down from one generation to the next for thousands of years. I possess a confidence that grows like a pearl within the hard shells of literature. I possess an immunity; I am protected by the steel armor of my books.

I am writing this in a prison cell.

But I am not in prison.

I am a writer.

I am neither where I am nor where I am not.

You can imprison me but you cannot keep me here.

Because, like all writers, I have magic. I can pass through your walls with ease.